What's Next . . . for You?

D0167048

What's Next . . . for You?

The Gussin Guide to Big Changes,
Big Decisions, & Big Fun

ROBERT AND PATRICIA GUSSIN

Oceanview Publishing
Ipswich, Massachusetts

ISBN: 978-1-933515-73-1

Published in the United States of America by Oceanview Publishing, Ipswich, Massachusetts
www.oceanviewpub.com

10 9 8 7 6 5 4 3 2 1

PRINTED IN THE UNITED STATES OF AMERICA

You are never too old to set another goal
or to dream a new dream.
— C. S. Lewis

This book is dedicated to
our children and grandchildren,
who always wonder what we'll do *next*.

Our thanks to Philip Kotler

This book is the result of a discussion with Dr. Philip Kotler, the S. C. Johnson Distinguished Professor of International Marketing at the Northwestern University Kellogg School of Management and one of the world's foremost experts on the strategic practice of marketing.

Phil, a neighbor in our condo complex in Longboat Key, Florida, buttonholed us after we gave a talk at our condo association gathering one winter evening in 2008. We'd been asked to speak because so many of our neighbors were dubious about our sanity when the word got out about our having drastically changed careers — in five years — from medical research and medicine to publishing suspense thrillers and growing grapes in New Zealand. So we put together a presentation, complete with slides — colorful ones of our awesome book covers and spectacular ones of our vineyards. Carrying our portable microphone, we headed to the clubhouse ballroom, amazed to see so many neighborly faces waiting.

There were lots of questions after the presentation, mostly about how and when and why we decided to make such big changes, and we answered them all. Pat and I usually, but not always, in agreement.

A couple of days later, Phil and Nancy Kotler strode up to us as we were having lunch on the outside deck of Mar Vista restaurant on Longboat Key. Why not, he suggested, jump into yet another ultrasuccessful next career! Take your "incredibly inspirational" story "on the road," he urged. After serious consideration, we decided to put our story — and, we hope, some inspiration — on the road. Between covers.

Thank you, Phil . . . off we go!

Thanks to all those people who have helped us along the way. There are far too many to list, family, friends, colleagues. And thanks to the gang at Oceanview Publishing for the encouragement and the tolerance and thanks to Ellen Count for a fabulous editing job.

What's Next . . . for You?

INTRODUCTION

Our transition from retirement to a new life—a more exciting new life than any we could possibly have imagined—didn't happen overnight, but came about piecemeal. And the venture into this life change has taken us in a direction far different and far beyond any we'd have dared to dream. If our story opens up new avenues of exploration for our readers, then that's our greatest hope.

All of us have to face change as we move along life's path, and it's how we embrace it or fear it that determines our future. No one lifestyle fits all, of course, and some of us leap at opportunities quicker and with less analyses than others. As we navigate new courses, the notion of *thoughtful impulsiveness*, which became revelatory for us, may also help you.

Friends and strangers have told us that the story we tell in *"What's Next . . . For You?"* has helped diminish the fear of jumping into something completely new. We're delighted that the book piques your curiosity. Of course, we aim to entertain — but perhaps also to inspire you to *un*retire to your own big decisions, big excitement, and big fun.

Chapter One

I hit the off button on the clock radio and struggled out of bed at five thirty a.m. I glanced across at Pat, asleep like a baby with the covers pulled almost all the way over her head. I wished I could sleep like that. I shook my head and trudged off toward the bathroom, dreading my ninety-minute drive from our Yardley, Pennsylvania, condo, to my New Brunswick, New Jersey, office on this dark, chilly mid-February morning.

We'd given in and moved about a year earlier, from a spacious contemporary house on three woodsy acres in Worcester to the new Yardley place. I *had* to shorten my drive, Pat insisted, by at least a half hour. We actually moved *farther* from her office, but now she could avoid crowded back roads and take the highways, so her trip time stayed about the same . . . forty-five minutes.

You may be wondering how we got into this horrendous commuting situation. It started in 1985 when we decided to move from our house in Hatboro, Pennsylvania, a house which had seen better days — before our rambunctious kids grew up there. That's when we stumbled across a beautiful contemporary house on three wooded acres in Worcester, and made a quick decision to buy it and move.

Actually, Pat stumbled across it when I was in Japan. She claimed to have read my mind from all the way across the Pacific; she was sure that I'd love the house so she signed on the dotted line. Then she held her breath until I got back. I can still hear her huge sigh of relief when I said I loved it, and I really did. With our two youngest sons, we moved out of the old neighborhood into the new.

The boys had to change school districts — a tragedy, they made clear — but the move hardly affected Pat's or my commute to our offices in two different suburbs of Philadelphia, each site a pleasant twenty-minute drive from our new home. I worked in Spring House as vice president for research and development at McNeil Pharmaceutical, and Pat in Fort Washington, as research and development vice president at McNeil Consumer Products.

But just a few weeks later, the parameters changed drastically when Jim Burke, the CEO and chairman of Johnson & Johnson, the parent company of our two McNeils, asked me to come to corporate headquarters in New Brunswick, New Jersey. That was when he offered me the job as corporate vice president for science and technology and chief scientific officer of Johnson & Johnson worldwide.

I'd oversee all the research and development efforts of the world's largest, most diversified healthcare company — several thousand scientists and physicians, all over the globe.

"This position will open the door for you," Jim Burke promised, "to every major university and research center in the world." The job also linked the Johnson & Johnson scientific community to the board of directors of the corporation. Overall, "the opportunity for interactions is endless."

This challenge was too good to turn down. I did hesitate because I was so happy at McNeil, but Pat informed me that if I refused that job it would convince her that I was totally insane. A very persuasive argument. And so, in early 1986, I began the nightmare commute: seventy miles and one and a half hours on the boring, congested Pennsylvania *and* New Jersey Turnpikes. Our move to Worcester actually had added another twenty miles — landing me squarely on the boys' side of the house controversy.

But, as usually happens, time passed — and we all adjusted. Our fourteen-year-old and twelve-year-old sons thrived in their new schools. Friends, parties, sports —

football, basketball, baseball all came to pass, and in fairly short order, the boys loved our house in the woods. I adjusted to my drive, as well, thanks to audio books. When had I ever been handed three hours a day to "read" for pleasure?

Early in my corporate career, I'd dutifully tried listening to educational stuff like business tapes and scientific and medical tapes, and even foreign language lessons, but often I found myself so sleepy that I had to pull off the road. So then I stocked up on mystery and thriller novels, they not only kept me awake, but occasionally I even drove past our house, I was so into the story. Pat said that she always knew when I was at an exciting part in a book because she would hear the car enter the garage, but I wouldn't come into the house for another five or ten minutes.

We lived in that house for twelve happy years. Then, by nineteen ninety-seven, the boys had gone on to college, none of our seven kids lived at home anymore — and here came *Pat's* big job change. In her new job as worldwide vice president of research and development for Johnson & Johnson Consumer Pharmaceuticals, she'd be responsible for all of J&J's over-the-counter pharmaceutical products research, spending time in many countries around the world to develop formulations and products to satisfy each country's needs and unique regulatory requirements. Though she'd keep her main office in Fort Washington,

Pennsylvania, she'd have to spend more time at the New Brunswick corporate headquarters, in central New Jersey. Since we were both now heading east and north, we figured that Yardley seemed like a good, convenient location. And did I mention that it was a townhouse? Not only an easier drive, but no more yard work. Oh, and by then two of our older sons had recycled to live at home. Too bad, boys, we're downsizing. Not enough room, time for you to move into your own places.

CHAPTER TWO

Tough daily commutes aside, we loved our jobs. Pat and I both had plenty of responsibility and plenty of freedom to lead our organizations. No complaints, except that both of us were travelling — sometimes together, but mostly separately. Sometimes we saw each other only as much as the time it took to repack our suitcases. Once we realized two days before separate business trips to Europe that each of us was scheduled to be in Paris on the same evening with reservations in separate hotels one street apart. We fixed that situation in a hurry. Imagine if we'd bumped into each other on the Champs Elysées or walking on the quays by the Seine.

When we weren't traveling, we spent weeknights in our Yardley condo, weekends at the beach house we'd decided on impulse to begin building in the summer of nineteen ninety-one, in Amagansett, New York. The small village of Amagansett is known as one of the Hamptons, the fabled celebrity summer refuge near the eastern end of the south shore of Long Island. Our white modern house sits among sand dunes facing the Atlantic Ocean. We're surrounded by two acres of beauty beyond words. Pat and I still can't believe the place is ours, and we joke about when will the real owners come and kick us out.

We were so anxious to spend time at the beach, that we developed a crazy routine to get us out there and back every weekend that we weren't traveling on business or pleasure. Late every Friday afternoon, we drove the 150 miles in some of the country's worst traffic. Pat would drive from her office in Fort Washington, Pennsylvania, to mine in New Brunswick. At about six-thirty, she parked her car in the Johnson and Johnson garage and we took off in mine for the remaining 100-mile drive to the Hamptons. We'd stop for a late dinner and arrive in our Amagansett neighborhood about eleven.

Then after a glorious stay on Saturday and Sunday, we would get up at three a.m. Monday and leave the house about three forty-five a.m. I drove empty roads about two and a half hours to New Brunswick while Pat snoozed. Then Pat would awaken, get in her car, and drive to her office in Fort Washington to arrive at eight a.m., just in time to start the workday. But I was early. Arriving around six-thirty a.m., I'd close my office door, lean back in my desk chair, feet on desk, and sleep till I heard people coming in between seven-thirty and eight o'clock. I'd get up, switch on the office fluorescents, open the door, and greet my colleagues as they arrived.

Getting to Amagansett and back was a little rough, but our weekends at the beach house were well worth it. We were sure happy to get to bed early on those Monday nights.

Sometimes when we think back to how we came to build our house in the dunes, we're struck by how impulsive we were and still are. We defend our approach by calling our decision-making style "thoughtful impulsiveness." It was 1991, we'd been enjoying a three-day July weekend, living the Hamptons life. Days on the sparkling sand beaches, evenings dining out, nights at the Southampton Inn, and mornings sleeping till whenever we woke up. The wide beaches, the quaint shops, all sorts of wonderful restaurants, the fascinating Hamptons people watching — were so seductive.

On that particular weekend on Friday night, over halibut for me and lobster for Pat at the unparalled Della Femina restaurant, we began talking about how perfect it would be to retire, someday, to that area. Pat said she liked it better than any other place that we had taken shore vacations, and I couldn't disagree. So, the next morning, we decided to drive around neighborhoods and try to get a feel for what *living* there really might be like. We didn't figure that the decision would have a dramatic impact on our lives.

Chapter Three

The lot was one of the greatest locations imaginable. Rolling sand dunes extended to a wide, pristine beach with that dazzling, nearly white sand meeting the waves of a sparkling blue-green ocean. At ten a.m. on Saturday, maybe half a dozen people were visible on the beach in the distance, both directions. We were enchanted by the beauty, the power and immensity of the ocean vista. A FOR SALE sign gave a realtor's phone number.

We took in our immediate surroundings. A beautiful contemporary house sat on the opposite side of a narrow boardwalk-style walkway that led to a set of wooden steps down to the beach. Another strikingly beautiful, white contemporary house sat behind the first, and another gray-tinged beauty behind that. All had generous lots with large spaces between the houses. Directly behind the lot on which we stood, we saw another empty lot with a SOLD sign — and behind that, a pretty, gray-shingled older house.

I looked at Pat and shrugged my shoulders. "Should I call?"

She was tentative, too. We did not intend to retire for ten to fifteen years, the location was a significant distance from our Pennsylvania house, and did not seem a feasible weekend shore spot. We already owned a house in Pennsylvania, and a small condo on the Gulf Coast in Florida, so we were neither financially nor mentally ready for another investment.

But this two-acre lot was spectacular. Magic. Could not have been more beautiful if it had been dropped from heaven before our eyes. We looked at each other for a couple of silent seconds, and I reached through the open car door for the phone.

We were at the location, I told the realtor, and found it appealing. I did my best not to jump up and down and tell her it was the most gorgeous property I'd ever seen — for fear she'd raise the price. I tried to keep my voice unemotional as I asked, How much? She was wiser. Come to her office, and we'd discuss it. She added that the parcel was the finest to come on the market in months and one of the very few remaining oceanfront properties in the Hamptons. I saw multiplying dollar signs as Pat and I drove off to her office.

The price? Worse even than I expected. I was living in

another world—a world long past. But I was stoic—no tears; I just told the realtor we would think about it and get back to her.

Saturday evening dinner at Bobby Van's restaurant in Bridgehampton was not a joyous occasion even though the food was delightful. I moped, Pat was practical. She shocked me by claiming that the property could be within our reach if we looked at it as an investment. I contended that if we bought the land, judging by the surrounding houses, we'd never be able to afford to build a house on it. The neighbors wouldn't appreciate a trailer or a tent, I joked. Pat, calm and logical as usual, said we could buy the lot—and keep it for ten years. The land surely would appreciate in value; and then, when we were close to retirement, we could decide whether to sell it or build a house. Sensible, but I continued sullen through the Sunday drive home.

Monday morning, I awoke with a flicker of optimism, and had barely walked into my office when I called the realtor. She'd told us the developer was in financial crisis and that was why the oceanfront gem now was for sale. He'd been keeping the property for himself, but as his finances deteriorated, had reluctantly put it on the market. Only the day before we called her, she announced—lucky for us, he'd *halved* the price to get a deal. That's why and how the price came *down* to the figure that'd all but knocked me out of my chair in her office that Saturday. In fact, she was telling the truth about the price history — confirmed soon after in a local news story that chronicled the developer's woes.

Anyway, I made a lowball offer. The realtor said she didn't think my bid would be acceptable, but that the development company board was to meet that morning, and she'd mention the figure. About four hours later, she called back and said no go, but they would consider a figure midway between my offer and the asking price. In an instant of manic insanity I said, "I'll take it."

She said she would fax a contract; we hung up. I felt like I didn't know whether to dance around the office or hide in the closet for fear of divulging my condition that could only have resulted from ingesting some psychedelic substance. I could barely hit the phone buttons to call Pat's office. Her assistant put me through. "We got it!" I shouted. Silence on the other end.

"We did? The lot?"

"Yes" — still shouting — "it's ours." Then I calmed down and replayed the details.

CHAPTER FOUR

For a year after we bought the Amagansett property, we made the drive to Long Island often, for weekends. We slept in hotels, but we spent hours sitting on our dune gazing at the ocean. We even bought French bread sandwiches and a bottle of wine and picnicked on the lot or on the beach. The high water mark was the property line — so the beach was our front- or backyard, depending on your point of view.

Logical thoughts, as often happens, give way to impulsive, illogical, even antilogical actions. At our first homeowners' association meeting, we met our six neighbors. Everyone was excited that all seven lots were now sold, and we had a complete community. As we talked, they encouraged, just about badgered, us to build sooner than we planned. In fact, they wanted us to build immediately. Our responses were vague. Little did they know that our plan was to wait ten years.

Then we made the impulsive move that started the snowball rolling downhill. Why not talk to an architect, we figured, just to get some ideas. That was in autumn, nineteen ninety-two, and our house was completed in April, nineteen ninety-four. So much for logical approaches and sensible plans. Not only did we build ten years early, but we went from a two bedroom oceanside cottage to a six-bedroom house — our family was growing, not only our children, but at that time seven grandchildren, too — and we put in a pool, apprehensive about little grandchildren swimming in the ocean. Good-bye to savings and hello to a big mortgage.

Looking back, our decision-making process involved much emotion and little logic. How did it turn out to be among the best decisions we ever made? There's something to be said for what eventually we began to call "thoughtful impulsiveness." Superficially, it's easy to conclude that Pat provides the thoughtfulness, and I add the impulsiveness, but, realistically, I'd say we each contribute some of both.

Since nineteen ninety-four, we've spent almost every weekend at the beach house; our children and grandchildren have a place to hang out and bond. Cousins really got to know each other and built lasting relationships. Ever since we retired, in February of two thousand, and sold our Pennsylvania property, we've lived half the year in Amagansett, and the other half in a lovely oceanfront

condominium on Longboat Key, Florida, a spectacular bar-
rier island off the coast of Sarasota on the Gulf of Mexico.
Guess which part of the year we live where!

Chapter Five

Now that you have some background, I can begin to try to explain how we got from careers in medicine and medical research to consulting in our corporate specialties to medical volunteering to the ownership of two vineyards — in New Zealand no less — and to starting a book publishing company. As Pat says, we went in the right direction, from medicine to books and wine. Not merely an editor and publisher, she even has written three mystery/thriller novels, and oh, by the way — I authored a humorous sports novel. The books are published, remain in print, and readers love them.

Now let me tell you the next part of the story, how we arrived at retirement in 2000. This was not one of our impulsive decisions, at least for me, but maybe for Pat as you'll see. It was traditional for a corporate officer at Johnson and Johnson to retire at age sixty-two. That ripe old age would be achieved by me in January of 2000. I thought that the auspicious year of 2000 would make it always easy to answer the question, "How long have you been retired?" Also, I would have just completed my twenty-sixth year with the company.

It all sounded pretty attractive to me, but one major obstacle existed — Pat. Being a few years younger than me, what would she want to do? She had a terrific job. Would she retire early? If not, we couldn't move to our oceanfront locations, and I would be left to wander about trying to think of something to do. But I knew that I could certainly stay in my job beyond 2000, if I wished.

So I presented my thoughts to Pat. To my great surprise and relief, she reacted pretty positively to the possibility of retirement on my time schedule, although she hated the word retirement. She did not commit immediately, for sure she was going to think about it. Before long she informed me that it sounded wonderful and exciting. We would "graduate," not retire, to a new segment of our life. But we still had about three years to wait. That was not easy even though we really liked our jobs.

That made us outright schizophrenic; we love our job; we love our ocean; we love being in warm weather; but what will we do next?

Now when we look back, to answer the question, "What's Next?" the *thoughtful impulsiveness* of the Hampton

house saga looks like the first chapter on the road to retirement and good practice for what was to come.

Chapter Six

During my time as corporate vice president for science and technology of Johnson &Johnson, I had many fascinating experiences. Near the top of that list was the opportunity to start a research group in Australia. I made several exploratory trips to the stunning city of Sydney, with its numerous bays and harbors and the fascinating array of boats visible from practically anywhere in the city. Then, in nineteen eighty-seven, I raided the University of New South Wales for one of their top scientists. I hired Dr. Denis Wade, an M.D.-Ph.D. with an international reputation as a scientist, but also as an entrepreneur and a leader, to shepherd the Australian group. All of Denis's prehire fanfare turned out to be hard fact. Denis built the organization into one of the world's finest molecular genetics laboratories. He rented space for the labs and outfitted them with state-of-the-art equipment, recruited a molecular genetics team from the government laboratories in

Canberra, and supplemented it with additional scientists hired from universities and other high-tech companies. On top of that, Denis has a dynamic personality and he's become a good friend.

From that point on, I had to make at least a few business trips a year to the group in Sydney. The city always charmed me with its beauty, and I couldn't wait to congratulate the research team on its progress toward drug and diagnostic product goals.

As I mentioned, Pat and I retired in February of two thousand. When Dr. Wade decided to retire in December 2002, we were invited to Sydney for the retirement festivities, and I was asked to be a keynote speaker. They didn't have to ask twice.

Why not take a side trip to New Zealand on our way to Australia? We'd heard so much about New Zealand's raw, natural beauty, but during the years that I went back and forth to Australia, we'd never had time to make the detour. And so we planned to drive around as much as we could of California-sized New Zealand in two and a half weeks before going on to Australia for a week. We'd been formally retired, but serving on boards of directors, volunteering in medicine, and actively consulting for two years — this was actually the first time we were able to appreciate the flexibility and diversity of the retirement lifestyle.

Amazingly, exploring New Zealand would be our first step in the disappearance of our retirement.

Chapter Seven

The early dawn approach by the Air New Zealand 747 to the airport in Auckland displayed hues of seasonal greens in the fields and forests and spectacular blues in the waters surrounding this magnificent modern city. Even after the thirteen-hour flight from Los Angeles, we were so excited we just dropped our bags in our hotel room and went off on foot to explore. Grand surprise! We'd arrived during America's Cup week, and Auckland was the site of the world's greatest sailing race. We even found a harbor cruise that allowed a real close-up look at the teams sailing their practice runs through the course. Exhilarating!

Eager to see all of a country as big as California, we took off early the next morning in our Toyota Rav 4 SUV, heading for the northern part of the North Island, which is slightly smaller than the South Island, but is home to two-thirds of the New Zealand population, with one million in or near Auckland. In the days that followed, we became more and more enchanted with both the urban and pastoral beauties of this country of about three and a half million people — and thirty million sheep. Every one of those three million folks whom we met was a paragon of friendliness. We drove through as much of the stunning North Island as we could in the first week, then took the three-hour ferry ride from Wellington to Picton on the northeast tip of the South Island. We spent the next week and a half exploring the South Island, one place more glorious than the next.

We fell in love not only with the unspoiled beauty of the country, but as well with the New Zealanders — Kiwi's, as they call themselves. But in particular, Pat fell hard for the glorious vineyards of the South Island. As we drove past vineyard after vineyard, Pat came up with a new mantra.

"Wouldn't it be fun to be in the wine business in New Zealand?" Pat asked

"Uh-huh," I replied.

Even after four or five days of my virtually ignoring her hints, she was not to be deterred. In pubs and inns, even in gas stations, she asked people about the wine industry. I must admit I quickly became fascinated by what they said.

In certain climatically ideal regions of the South Island, grape growing for wine had taken on the intensity of the California gold rush. Everyone grew grapes.

Accountants, doctors, clerks, taxi drivers — anyone with a garden was tearing it out and planting grapes. Fruit farmers had replaced acres and acres of cherry and apple trees with grapevines. The farmers had no trouble calculating that a ton of wonderful wine grapes was worth a lot more than a ton of apples or cherries.

By the time we flew to Sydney for the retirement party, I'd been so mentally battered by my spouse that I'd actually begun thinking in earnest about the New Zealand wine business. As fate would have it, one of the scientists in the J&J Sydney genetics lab came from a family that had grown grapes in Australia for about fifty years, and was a major supplier of grapes to the Australian wine industry.

At the reception for Denis Wade, I pulled Wayne Gerlach aside, "Pat is driving me crazy about our getting into the wine business in New Zealand. What do you think?" Unwittingly, I'd just taken another large step in the opposite direction from our retirement.

Wayne's mind could have been a clone of Pat's . . . *probably one of the hottest investment opportunities,* he allowed, *in the hemisphere!* His sister, a master's degree oenologist, no less, had left Australia and moved to New Zealand to become a winemaker for one of the largest New Zealand wineries. He suggested that a reasonable way for Pat and me to get into the New Zealand wine business would be simply to buy part of a vineyard. He recommended that we *not* buy a winery because you had to *know* wine making, as well as be versed in import-export technicalities. But if you bought a vineyard, or a piece of one, you could just contract with established professional groups to manage it and you could sell your grapes to a winery.

Then my colleague delivered the knockout punch. Wayne said he would put us in touch with his sister by e-mail. We could describe our interests to her and just see where things went. She could give us some good advice. Why not?

Three months later, we owned a forty-acre vineyard in the Marlborough region, the premier grape-growing area in New Zealand. Already in its fourth year since planting, our new venture was ready to produce its first vintage.

Not only was the vineyard itself scenically beautiful, but when you stand in it and look east, about two hundred yards away you see the South Pacific Ocean — and between the vineyard and the ocean, a view of sheep grazing in a paddock. To the west, you see a distant snow-capped mountain — even though the year-round temperature in the vineyard pretty much calls for shirtsleeves. Directly behind the vineyard we christened, "Oceanview," to the north is a small mountain — hike to the top and you can look down on our vineyard and all the vineyards for miles around. To the east, across the azure water of Clifford Bay, on a clear day you can see the southern tip of New Zealand's North Island. The coastline south of the vineyard is edged by steep palisades of white limestone-like rocks. Yes, they do remind us of Britain's famed cliffs of Dover!

Oceanview is the last vineyard before our road ends at the ocean, just where the Awatere River empties into Clifford Bay. The spot is like an exclamation point to the beauty of the area.

The entire Marlborough region is enchantingly serene. Vineyards fill the plains and rolling hills for mile after mile, a striking contrast with the often snow-peaked mountain ranges that surround the wine country. Add the turquoise Pacific Ocean to the east and the variety of lakes and rivers in Marlborough — and you have a painting created by God, the artist. All of this natural beauty is complemented by the occasional simplistic town. No wonder they chose this country as the setting for *Lord of the Rings*.

Our villa — which is not as fancy as the name implies — is just outside Blenheim, the largest and busiest town in the area. Still, with a population of about thirty thousand, Blenheim isn't that big, and reminds us of U. S. small towns in the nineteen forties and fifties. Shops are mostly privately owned, not chains; folks are open and friendly to strangers and generally give us that "good people" feeling. When we're there, we don't want to leave, but we're eight thousand miles from our children and grandchildren, so we don't plan to live there full time.

Hello grapes . . . good-bye retirement. A big chunk of

retirement, anyway. We'd have to work a lot harder to completely unretire. But we've never regretted the vineyard decision — or the other big changes to come.

Why, you may ask, didn't we buy a California vineyard, or one in the wine country not far from our Long Island home? Two reasons. First, we love New Zealand, and the vineyard gives us an excuse to keep going back. Second, and probably more important, in California or Long Island, we'd only have been able to afford a parcel of land that could produce enough grapes each fall to fill our fruit bowl.

Chapter Eight

You may think I'm always blaming Pat for pushing us into new projects, like the Amagansett house and our Oceanview Vineyards in New Zealand. Actually, I never can thank her enough for propelling stodgy me into new terrain. I must admit that the farther I moved out of my safe little comfort zone, the easier it seemed to get. But Pat was not finished nudging me toward the abyss.

It all started in nineteen ninety-eight about two years before we retired, Pat had been promoted to Johnson & Johnson worldwide vice president for consumer pharmaceutical research and development. Big title, bigger job. The assignment covered a lot of territory, literally, and took Pat far afield, including to China and Japan. Now, as she will tell you, and I can attest from my own experience, you can work from your briefcase for two to three hours on a flight before you zone out or fall asleep from boredom. So those trips to the Far East, especially if you've already seen the movies, leave you with nine or ten hours to fill. If you can't sleep, what do you do? Pat found herself spending much of that time letting memories flood her consciousness — especially some from all those years ago in medical school.

When she started med school at Wayne State University in Detroit, Pat already had two sons, ages three years and three months. During her four years of medical training, she had two more children and, as she will tell you, never missed a class. But, preoccupied with the heavy workload of her studies, and with caring for a family, she did not spend her time profoundly thinking about the social-economic upheaval that the city of Detroit underwent in nineteen sixty-seven.

Many years later, during those long business flights, she became obsessed with memories of those tumultuous times in Detroit. Pat herself — now a novelist — will tell you how that evolved.

CHAPTER NINE

For thirty years of my adult life, children, a husband and a medical career, consumed every minute of my everyday existence, and it wasn't until I found myself on far-flung flights out of JFK to Tokyo, Beijing, or Shanghai, that I realized for the first time anywhere, that I had hours of uninterrupted time.

Now, on my way to Bangkok, I think it was, I pulled out a yellow legal pad, and let myself travel back mentally to Detroit in nineteen sixty-seven, the year of the devastating Detroit riots, and the year I started medical school. I was a mother coping with the demands of small children and a daunting curriculum. On a professional level, I was staring life and death in the face every day at the hospital. But on another level, I was at the epicenter of social upheaval and in the crucible of poverty, destruction, hopelessness, hate, and fear.

When I started my scratching on that yellow pad, all

those years later during the long-haul flights, I mused on the different worlds of Detroit when I was in med. school — the contrast of the extreme poverty with my own busy life of middle-class privilege. And I decided that I wanted to interweave these two disparate strains in a fictional way.

What gradually appeared on the notepad pages were the stories of three families and a main character, much like myself back then, Laura Nelson. Laura starts medical school in Detroit amid the riots. She has a husband and two sons, Mikey, a three-year-old, and Kevin, the three-month-old baby; no coincidence, the ages of my sons at that time.

But that's where the similarity stops between Laura's life and my own. Unlike me, Laura experiences the riots in a very personal way when she confronts a violent crime. The choices she makes produce devastating consequences that will shadow her forever. When *Shadow of Death* ends, the reader is left with the question: Is Laura a *victim* or a *vigilante*?

At first, telling this story as a thriller was not a conscious decision, but as the plot started to come to me, danger and suspense took over the tale. In the setting, I wanted the reader to take away a better appreciation of social issues that haunted — and still haunt — our cities; a sense of juggling family and career, and a close-up feel for medical education in the late nineteen sixties.

Shadow of Death eventually was nominated by the International Thriller Writers Association as 2006 Best First Novel. And two universities have used the novel as a text in contemporary urban history at Michigan State University, and in sociology at Duquesne University to prepare students for community service. I still find all three of these unexpected outcomes most humbling.

Never in my most outlandish dreams had I planned to be a writer, and I never had a clue as to where this early shot at writing would lead. But once I'd completed *Shadow of Death*, I knew I would continue writing. I had stumbled into something I loved.

Chapter Ten

The second scariest moment of my life was when I learned that Pat was going to write a novel. Everyone wants to write a book, and hardly any have the talent or energy to do it. And of those who try, many fail miserably. How do you tell your wife not to quit her day job?

Not only did she inform me on that fateful day of her intention to write a novel, but she handed me a sheaf of about twenty handwritten pages. My sheer terror surely showed on my face, but with as blank an expression as I could manage, I announced, "I would prefer to wait until you have written a hundred or a hundred and fifty pages, rather than to read just short snippets." But reasoning was, she'll never get that far. She'll get immersed in other things, and give up on this crazy idea.

She shrugged and walked away in the direction of her messy home office, with pages firmly in hand. I sighed with relief, my shoulders relaxed, and I headed off to the

kitchen to pour myself a glass of sauvignon blanc to cele-
brate my successful delaying tactic, certain that I had seen
the end of that project.

A few months later on the evening of a violent thun-
derstorm, Pat thrust at me a thick stack of pages — the
first several chapters of her embryonic novel. The *most*
frightening moment of my life had arrived. Time to read
the product of her efforts.

My shoulders slumped, my breathing shallow and
rapid, head bowed, I plodded to my home office at the
opposite end of the house from Pat's, dropped the stack of
papers on my cluttered desk and sat down. I leaned my
elbows on the desk, hands on my forehead, eyes closed, and
prayed. But when I opened my eyes, the manuscript was
still there. No help from any higher power. And so I faced
the inevitable. I turned on the reading lamp, and stared at
page one. Maybe the storm would knock out the lights and
I'd have a reprieve.

The shock came fast and profound, I probably paled.
Pat's writing was really strong. The story was compelling.
I couldn't turn the pages fast enough. Was this written by
the same person I've known for so many decades? Of
course, Pat was extremely *smart;* she did have a good imagination, and had written scientific and medical articles.
Yes, she could write, but she'd never revealed till now this
side of her imagination and literary style. The story
enthralled me, and the characters did what you always

hope they will — jump off the page. When I finished the last page of the stack, I had to keep from running down the hall to get her to tell me the rest of the story. Now I headed to the kitchen to pour myself another glass of the sauvignon blanc. This time I even poured a pinot noir for Pat.

CHAPTER ELEVEN

With encouragement from me and our children and friends who gamely read the developing manuscript, Pat became more confident and even more determined to stay the course. She wrote day after day, and I saw another activity track materializing for her in our "retirement" years.

I was thrilled for Pat. I was happy to see the results as she polished and finished her novel. When she went so far as to ask me to edit her work, and then accepted some of my editing advice, I felt great. She obviously enjoyed writing fiction. I could tell she felt energized by the chance to stretch her imagination and create characters and situations from her own right brain. A far cry from writing medical reports and papers, where you only can state facts and describe observations.

Pat took so well to this newfound vocation, she periodically admonished me to take a shot at writing a novel, too. No, thanks. I stood fast in my lack of desire and undoubted lack of talent for fiction. I was busy and happy with my job-related activities, I loved collaborating with other scientists, and had no trouble whiling away any spare time in our modern kitchen — cooking. Yep, you heard right, *cooking*. Me, the macho male, now with saucepan and wooden spoon in hand.

After we built the Hamptons' house, I took up grilling for the droves of friends and family who came to spend weekends with us. I discovered that I really enjoyed experimenting with the different types of marinades I concocted for chicken or tuna or steak, and I enjoyed grilling for a crowd.

Then, one day when several of our kids were visiting, my plans to grill chicken were thwarted by a rainstorm that wouldn't let up. Forced to cook indoors — something I'd never done — I marinated the chicken in a mix of zesty Italian herbal salad dressing and red wine vinaigrette salad dressing, and after letting the chicken parts sit in the marinade about three hours in the fridge, I transferred them to the broiler. Revelation! Best chicken I've ever eaten. Pat and the kids agreed — and that day Pat unceremoniously retired from the kitchen. She still claims that this may well have been the best day of her life.

Now I cook all our meals and I really get a kick out of it. Maybe after a career in scientific experimentation or as a function of some artistic part of my brain, hard to know, but anyway, I refuse to use recipes. I do read cookbooks for ideas, but that's it. I mix things that I think will taste good together. We still do eat out a lot, so I've tasted many cuisines and dishes, and I have some idea of what should go well together. And so I experiment.

Must be the scientist at work, because I still refer to marinating as *incubating*. As in most scientific endeavors, some experiments do fail. Pat is most kind, however — and so thankful not to be cooking, that she'll eat whatever I cook and compliment the chef. But I have done a few culinary experiments I couldn't eat, and of course, wouldn't put on her plate, either.

Over time, I've become more daring. From broiled steak, chicken, and fish, I've advanced to chili, veal scaloppini *Robert* (French pronunciation, please — or make that *Gussini*, more Italian), spaghetti squash marinara, and the best lamb chops and California roast I ever have tasted. These are just a few of my experiments. Now, I jokingly, refer to myself not as a chef or cook, but as a "food impressionist" — a Monet of the kitchen.

Something interesting happened when I first cooked lamb. I remembered the lamb chops, served rare, that I almost sent back to the kitchen in a Moroccan restaurant in Paris. I'd been so reluctant even to taste them. But the chops turned out to be the best I'd ever eaten. So when I first tried cooking lamb, I broiled it medium rare on the rare side. Fearing that when Pat saw how red it was, she wouldn't eat it, I set the table, lit candles, and turned off the lights. She loved the dish. She no longer orders lamb in a restaurant because she says it can't compare.

The other lasting effect of that first lamb dinner is that ever since that night, when we eat at home, we dine by candlelight. Great food, candlelight, soft music. A romantic evening at home with the "food impressionist."

But these blissful moments were not to last forever.

Chapter Twelve

Before we retired, Pat's writing was limited to the minimal spare time she had at home, and to some of those hours on the long flights. She also managed to squeeze in a few weekends at writers' conferences. These were fun, she met a lot of authors, learned to sharpen her skills, and she acquired professional insights into the publishing world. After we retired, with more free time at her disposal, Pat not only was able to get in more writing hours, but went to more of the writers' meetings and symposia that she said helped her work. Would she end up escorting me, sort of kicking and screaming, to one of those events? Let's hear what Pat has to say.

Back to the yellow notepads that always went with me on those intercontinental flights. Eventually, they started to stack up beside the bed where I'd stashed them. One day,

I realized that they'd become a safety hazard. I could hardly get out of bed without slipping on paper. Now I know that in that first draft, I probably had enough material for three novels. I wrote and wrote. But to what end? Nobody, including me, can read my handwriting!

After the time I tripped over a toppling stack, I realized I had to make a major decision. Either get all those words into a word processor or consign the pads to an incinerator. After procrastinating as long as I could, I faced reality. I needed to get computer literate; beyond just answering simple e-mails, I had to learn how to create a document—and crucially—how to save a document. At my real job, I'd been blessed with an excellent secretary, but now I was on my own.

So I plunged in. Endless hours, struggling to decipher my handwriting, watching in horror as document after document disappeared in faulty computer maneuvers. Those were trying times for me—and for my family, but eventually they became immune to my howls of frustration when I "lost" a document. Thankfully for them, most of our kids were off at college by that time, and missed the histrionics. But this couldn't have been an easy time for Bob. At last, I mastered the most important lesson: how to save and how to save in the right place so you can find that chapter again!

After the miserable data-entry exercise came the next and even harder hurdle—editing. Suffice it to say that much of what was in those notebooks ended up on the cutting room floor. *Shadow of Death*, as published, is version "M," the result of lots of editing, brutal editing. The real champion editor is Bob, who, over a ten-year period, read each version and offered his opinion. I learned that I have very thick skin. I deeply appreciate criticism and feel honored that others would give their valuable time to help me.

My second novel, *Twisted Justice*, was not scrawled on notepads, but was by now quite expertly entered directly into a computer. Today, I'm smug about my computer skills, but only after enduring the agony of defeat. *Twisted Justice* again features Laura Nelson. Seven years after her medical school graduation, she's a thoracic surgeon in Tampa, Florida. She has five children now; her husband, no longer a social worker, anchors the nightly news, and is a local celebrity. The rest is a mystery I won't reveal here. But more important to me than plot gymnastics in *Twisted Justice*, is that readers come away with a greater appreciation of the complexity of family dynamics, and a sense of just how fragile and precarious life can be.

My third novel, *The Test*, begins like a family saga, but quickly becomes a psychological thriller. After the Parnell family patriarch dies, his offspring must take a "moral values test" to determine the distribution of his billion dollar estate. The fictional family is complicated and diverse, unwieldy, and unpredictable. Without living in our own large family, I don't think I could have written this novel. Each family is unique and always evolving; for the Parnell family the evolution erupts into a thriller of an outcome.

I know several people who hve struggled with inheritance decisions; their predicaments inspired *The Test*. Another near and dear inspirational source influenced the nature of 'the test' I dreamed up — the Johnson & Johnson "Credo" — modified to guide the Parnell siblings rather than the philosophy of a corporation.

In my next novel, tentatively titled *Abduction*, also a thriller, two of three nine-year-old identical triplets are kidnapped. This time, I strive for the emotional impact not only of the most devastating of parental terrors, but the overwhelming anguish of the remaining safe child.

Members of the Jones family and the Monroe family from *Shadow of Death*, return in *Abduction* as Katie Jones and Scott Monroe are the parents of the triplets.

For all my readers who have asked whether Laura Nelson of *Shadow of Death* and *Twisted Justice* will return as a main character — the question I hear most frequently — the answer is, yes. At least, I hope so.

I've grown to love writing, but an author's life is not all fun and games. It is isolated work, yes, but it's not the solitude that bothers me. Quite the opposite. The dark side, for me, is all the promotion we're obliged to do. Every author has to promote, promote, promote. I'd rather do anything but get out there and promote my book. What does it entail? All my least favorite chores. Contact bookstores, libraries, ask for book signings, ask to talk at reader-oriented gatherings, and on and on. Bob is the one who likes to give speeches, always has, and he's good. Not me, I'm more a backroom person. True, I do like to call the shots, but I don't like to be out there *performing*. Nevertheless, all this speaking and signing goes with the author territory.

Hold on a minute, I do like talking to people one on one, so when I'm at a bookstore event, I really enjoy meeting and greeting perfect strangers. When you're in your hometown and all your friends come to support you and buy your book, you feel pretty darn good. But when you're where nobody's ever heard of you, and everybody has a million other ways to spend their time and their money on any given night, the experience can be quite a downer. You arrive to an empty cluster of chairs — just you, a stack of your books and a nervous bookseller. You sit and chat with the store owner or manager, hoping against hope that a crowd will suddenly materialize. Fortunately, folks usually do show up, and most book signings, if not exactly fun, are productive. In sum, life on the promotional runway can be exhilarating although at times, humiliating.

So much for my writing career to date.

Jumping ahead, when eventually I found myself editor in chief of Oceanview Publishing, all my own awkward, even embarrassing, experiences have made me a good cheerleader for Oceanview authors as they take to the road to, yes, promote their books.

I give them the same advice I give myself. Talk to as many people as you can, make friends with the booksellers, and when it's all over, go home or to your hotel and have a glass of wine. Funny, there's an obvious synergy between books and wine.

Chapter Thirteen

Pat clearly had moved fiction writing to her post-retirement priority. She tackled writing with the same energy and verve she displays in everything she does. Determined to succeed as a novelist, she did. But the vortex she created with that unbridled energy eventually pulled me in another totally unanticipated direction.

You'll recall how Pat innocently urged me to attend writers' conferences with her, just to keep her company. Well, just to be with her, I did go along, and I patiently listened to one author, or wannabe author, after another, make presentations on everything from their approach to writing and their writing style to character development, to the trials and tribulations of finding a agent — not to mention a publisher. I admit I did sneak in a few naps while sitting in folding chairs at writers' meetings. Then, after several months, an unexpected thing — another one — happened.

Pat and I attended a local book signing and presenta-tion by Carl Hiaasen, the established and successful mys-tery author, whose tongue-in-cheek humor I thoroughly enjoyed.

About a week later, I went with Pat to a nearby week-end mystery writers' conference at the Sarasota Hyatt Hotel. In one of the sessions, I listened to two Florida-based mystery writers, Randy Wayne White and Tim Dorsey, whose style reminded me of Hiaasen's.

They, too, were great presenters, quick witted and entertaining. As I listened to them, something totally shocking happened to me. I suddenly had a burning desire to write a novel. I was stunned. I couldn't believe that my brain had turned on me. I went from an absolute lack of interest in writing fiction to wanting to get out of that meeting and get started. Had I developed acute schizo-phrenia?

We walked out of that session, and I said to Pat, "I am going to write a novel."

"What? You are?"

"Yes, I've decided to write a humorous mystery with an underlying serious message — like Florida writers Hiaasen and Dorsey." These and other Florida writers often incorpo-rate social issues into their stories, in many cases environ-mental issues. Perhaps because Florida is a quite environ-mentally conscientious state. So that's what I decided to do. I left the meeting determined and confident.

* * *

I couldn't wait to get started. When we got home, I grabbed a pen and a yellow pad like Pat's when she started, and rushed to my desk, where I sat and pondered. The environmental aspect of my novel-to-be preoccupied me. Global warming? Global cooling? What did I know about either? How could I make those topics funny!

What about pollution, litter, and trash? The lightbulb went on. Trash! Right! My brain kicked into sports mode — *Trash Talk*. I consider myself an avid sports fan, but Pat goes further. She claims I'm a sports fanatic and will watch any sporting event that comes along, no coaxing required.

Trash talk, the insulting banter that athletes use nowadays as a tactic to distract and intimidate their opponents. What if a bunch of athletes went to a symposium entitled, "Trash Talk," thinking it would hone their insult slinging techniques, but found an environmental meeting with topics such as recycling and waste hauling? The resulting culture clash of professional athletes and dedicated environmentalists could create a funny situation, indeed. And provided me, the aspiring author, a chance to insert into a humorous story some serious messages about environmental issues and about human interactions.

Several months of intensive writing resulted in my first novel, *Trash Talk*. I laughed while I wrote it, Pat laughed when she read it, but I never did make it a mystery. Some of our friends were willing to read it; they laughed a lot and enjoyed it. I took the manuscript and cheerfully tossed it in the nearest desk drawer. Mission accomplished.

"What?" Pat prompted. "Let's see it in print!"

The notion of a published *Trash Talk*, and what happened in the months that followed, wrote a whole new chapter in our lives — and turned out to be a giant step away from our retirement.

CHAPTER FOURTEEN

Joining the hordes of wannabe published authors was not my ambition, but now I found myself rather more interested in accompanying Pat to writers' conferences. While she absorbed advice on how to improve your writing skills, I became fascinated with the plight of writers struggling to find a publisher, or, when published, to get the support they wanted and needed from their publishers.

Meeting after meeting, I heard the same themes. *I've been rejected by twenty, thirty, forty, a hundred, publishers. I can't get an agent. I sent out zillions of letters, but no one will represent me, and publishers won't read an unagented manuscript.*

Yet, as they described their books-to-be, all but convinced that the book-to-be *never* would be, many of these writers seemed very talented. I became something between upset and depressed for them. Another theme: major publishers kept publishing the same few authors who, somehow, had gotten the big break and become so successful.

The hopefuls urged anyone listening to just take a look at the bestseller lists: week after week, month after month, the same authors. Of course, rare was the admission that perhaps the talent of these few could have accounted for the difference. Still, I suspected that among this horde of hopefuls, were real talent and many fine books that would never be read if something did not change.

Then, at one fateful meeting, while Pat went to a session on *How to Develop Your Characters*, I decided to attend one on self-publishing.

I listened to all the presentations. The upside was that your book got published — by you. Downsides? No way for you to distribute the book. Reviewers wouldn't deign to review it. Precious little respect from anyone but perhaps your family, and limited book sales out of your own car trunk. But the session did provide me with some idea of what's required to publish and sell a book.

When Pat and I met after our sessions ended, I hit her with the bombshell that would blow the rest of our retirement to smithereens. "I'm going to start a publishing company." A few little words — from me this time — that doubtless would change our life. Again.

Pat's mouth dropped; speechless for a few moments, she slowly shook her head back and forth, as though to clear her mind or her eardrums.

Oooh, and *wow*, came Pat's response. *"That's* interesting." I knew her. She already was fascinated, all but hooked, by the idea.

I recounted what I'd heard at the self-publishing session, while assuring her that I did not want to be a self-publisher. But after listening to so many unhappy writers, I thought I could do better for a small number of them than what they were getting, or not getting, from the big publishers.

As Pat and I headed to the hotel restaurant for lunch, she informed me that her book would be the first one published by the new company. I was pleased with her courage and confidence, but I tried hard to dissuade her. Pat had a successful New York agent representing her, and I was certain she would get picked up by a major publisher. I also pointed out that publishing hers as our first book would certainly seem like self-publishing. But she was not to be dissuaded.

"If you happen to make some mistakes on your first published book, I'd want you to make them with mine and not with an outside author's." How could I argue with that?

And so, *Shadow of Death* was to be the first product of Oceanview Publishing, Inc. The company name came easily. We'd dubbed our first vineyard in Marlborough, New Zealand, Oceanview because its vines flourish just a few hundred yards from the Pacific.

Following the *thoughtfully impulsive* decision to start a publishing company, the weeks and months were a whirlwind of activity. I made two key moves that set our future course, and moved us toward finally slamming the door on our retirement.

CHAPTER FIFTEEN

Two phone calls set our publishing destiny.

The first was to Warren Phillips, retired chairman of Dow Jones and retired publisher of the *Wall Street Journal*. Warren and his wife, Barbara Phillips, an editor, own Bridge Works Publishing in Bridgehampton, New York, not far from our place in Amagansett. They'd started the company after *their* first retirement. I'd never met Warren, but a mutual friend told us about the Phillips's and their enterprise, so I made a cold call, introduced myself, and told Warren of my idea. I will never forget his response. "Why would you want to do that? It's hard work, and you probably will never make any money."

Those encouraging words ringing in my ears, I plunged ahead, offering more detail on my reasons for wanting to try publishing. Would he be willing to give me a little guidance? The next day, over lunch in a quiet corner of a small restaurant in Bridgehampton, Pat and I eagerly picked Warren's and Barbara's brains.

The second call was to a longtime colleague and great friend, Susan Greger. Sue and I had worked together at Johnson & Johnson for more than twenty-five years. She was the director of outside programs in the corporate office of science and technology, but I'd heard recently that she was contemplating early retirement. When she answered my call, I wasted no time on pleasantries. "Sue, when you retire, do you want to go brain dead, or would you rather be a partner in a publishing company?"

Silence rang in my ears. I'm certain she figured I'd entered my own dotage a touch early. She apparently recovered, and inquired as to where the conversation was going. I gave her my entire pitch — reasons, opportunities, germinating thoughts and plans. My best hard-sell job. She said she'd think about it, and call me back. She did call, the next day, and agreed, with — let's call it, measured enthusiasm. P.S., she did not want to work full time after retirement. Fine, I said, I was thinking of only forty to fifty hours a week. She started to protest, but I laughed, and said about half time should be fine. Our Johnson & Johnson years had involved some brutal work schedules, so I know she didn't believe me, but she said okay. Hooked. I told her she would bring tremendous skills in process- and project-management and all the operational aspects of the business.

Three weeks later, Sue came to our house on Long Island, and we three partners began our planning process.

Not only are Warren and Barbara Phillips extremely nice people, but they talked us through every aspect of publishing. From the author contract to the editing process to getting books printed, distributed and sold, and everything in between. As a follow-up, they called and introduced us to an outstanding production group, and a distributor, who otherwise never would have agreed to work with us. In fact, I know that without that nudge from the Phillips's, neither organization even would have considered taking on a new company run by three people with no publishing industry experience.

I don't think we could have got the business off the ground without all that help and education from Warren and Barbara. The "godparents" of Oceanview Publishing not only continue to mentor and guide us, but they also have become good friends.

Chapter Sixteen

Our first publishing planning meeting was a three-day affair that reminded us of our Johnson & Johnson lives. Pat, Sue, and I toiled at the dining room table from morning to night. Fortified by coffee, bagels, soda, chips, and other snacks, we scribbled and flipped our flipcharts. We argued, joked, screamed at each other, planned and replanned. Just like the old days! We broke down every element of book publishing we figured we needed to account for; we discussed the when, where, and how to accomplish each. We planned to follow up with visits to the businesses where the Phillips's had introduced us.

In the late evenings, we drank wine and went out to dinner and drank more wine. Our uninhibited brains allowed additional thoughts and discussions about our future. Should we publish nonfiction as well as fiction? Should we concentrate on mysteries and thrillers and suspense, or be more general? We had a great, exhausting time. And at the end of three days, we had dozens of Magic Marker scribbled flipchart pages: activities and plans and assignments and dates.

From retirement, Pat and I had taken a high dive into a total-immersion pool of work. And of course, Sue's retirement had just begun. But, at the end of those three fateful days, both old and new retirees vanished, replaced by book publishing executives.

The sequel to the planning phase began in Arlington, Massachusetts, with our visit to Susan Hayes Associates, the book production group to which Warren Phillips introduced us. Before Susan started her company, she had worked in the book publishing industry for many years and for many of the largest publishers, including Little, Brown. Susan in turn provided a tutorial for the three of us, in what is required to produce a book. We struggled to ask some semi-intelligent questions. The quality and the amount of information she conveyed was top drawer. Still more astonishing, Susan agreed in principle to produce our books. Soon thereafter, we had a contract, and we had a production group, another mentor — and soon, another good friend.

While all our planning and organization proceeded, I got in touch with authors I'd met at some of those writers' conferences I'd dutifully attended. After a few weeks, I'd concluded verbal agreements with two of them to publish their books with us. Now, including Pat's book, we had a list of three. Amazingly, both of the two other authors I'd engaged already had published several books with major publishers. But, intrigued with our plans and our desire to do more for authors than had been done for them in the past, the two were willing to give us a try. A local independent bookstore, Circle Books, on St. Armands Circle in Sarasota, introduced us to the fourth author on our list. The bookstore owners loved his self-published work, and thought he'd be better off with us — and that his espionage thriller would be a great fit for Oceanview. Those predictions turned out to be right on target.

So, with four potential authors and a production group signed up, we were primed for our first visit to Warren Phillips's other resource: a company that could distribute our books.

CHAPTER SEVENTEEN

Arriving at the center of the publishing universe, Manhattan, we wore business suits, and in my case, a tie, and toted our briefcases to our meeting at Midpoint Trade Books. We felt almost as though we were back at Johnson & Johnson. That familiar feeling grew stronger when we sat down around a large conference table in a meeting room surrounded by offices. I especially enjoyed the good, we-can-handle-this feeling because in our new venture, I knew I could handle *most* tasks while wearing my comfortable, work-at-home tee shirt and shorts.

Founder and president of Midpoint, Eric Kampmann, and several of his staff, explained how the distribution system works, and what a publisher must provide. They showed us their catalog, pointing out some of the publishers they represent. They distribute to the major national bookstore chains, as well as to the major book wholesalers, who then sell to independent bookstores and to libraries.

We easily understood the importance of distribution. At our stage of development in the publishing business, we had no place to warehouse thousands of copies of books, and no way to ship them to booksellers all over the country — let alone to foreign locations.

Midpoint could be our warehouse and shipper, and even handle billing and collections, as well as the dreaded book returns. Now we learned the toughest lesson in the book business: if books aren't sold, they're returnable by stores and wholesalers at anytime. Returned merchandise may significantly affect initial sales numbers — result: an accounting nightmare. If we had to handle this part of the business ourselves, our new company would need an entire financial section.

We also would have to depend on a distributor to sell our books to the big chains, where small publishers do not have direct access. And we'd need the distributor to play a significant role with independent bookstores, too — to complement our own sales people, when we hired some.

Once again, at Midpoint, we were tutored. But as we gained a greater understanding of how the business worked, we began to learn faster and more easily. The recommendation from Warren Phillips, plus Midpoint execs' confidence in our business skills based on our Johnson & Johnson background, added up to an agreement with Midpoint to be our distributor. A few weeks later, we signed the contract. I managed to do that at home, wearing my shorts and tee.

With a production group, a distributor, and four authors under our belt, I was beginning to feel Oceanview was a real publishing company!

Momentum and confidence are wonderful things, and the three of us were gaining both. Suddenly, the organizing process seemed to get easier. But how were we to tell the world about Oceanview?

The Midpoint people had offered the name of a publicist whom they highly regarded, and suggested we call her. Pat and I also had met publicists at Book Expo in Chicago. A few months earlier, we'd been able to take in that largest U.S. book convention of the year — conveniently scheduled that year, to begin on the same date as a hospital board meeting we already were committed to attend in Chicago.

Book Expo was a daunting experience, with enough buyers and sellers to fill the huge Chicago convention center, McCormick Place. Publishers' booths by the hundreds. Printers, book jacket designers, agents, authors, bookstore owners and managers, and among still others, publicists. Just by observing all the variety of specialists bustling around the four-day meeting, you could see what it takes to publish a book.

On our return home to Amagansett, we interviewed

some New York publicists, but eventually we decided to work with Maryglenn McCombs in Nashville, whom Midpoint had recommended. What a great decision! Maryglenn has hundreds of business buddies in the press, plus magical writing skills — and she has the greatest southern drawl ever. Some days, I phone her just to hear her talk. On top of all that, she is nice as pie. A most experienced publicist, Maryglenn has a background in other aspects of publishing, as well. Once again, we gained a teacher, a mentor, and a friend — as well as a publicist. Another bonus: Maryglenn's husband, Tim, happens to be an intellectual property attorney specializing in the entertainment business. When he's not competing in a triathlon, we can go to him for advice and counsel.

We were on a roll, and we scored once again when we were introduced to a book jacket designer in Iowa, George Foster. One of the top jacket designers in the industry, he's one of the most creative persons I've met. His talent is apparent on the jackets of Oceanview books.

Sue Greger has a special knack for recruiting talented friends and acquaintances to work with us. She added Mary Adele Bogdon to our team. A longtime pharmaceutical sales representative with McNeil Consumer Products Company, Mary Adele brought her sales capabilities to Oceanview and quickly segued from pharmaceuticals to books. Now we had a sales force of one, but one with great energy. Mary Adele not only visited and phoned booksellers, but also arranged book signings at the stores for our authors.

Sue recruited another friend, Joe Hall, for our information technology needs. Joe was able to help us out on weekends and evenings and designed our Web site, as well as our business computer systems. Sue even succeeded in drafting her sister, Sandy, to manage our data files after hours — she's a full-time occupational therapist.

Later, we were fortunate to add two other wonderful members to our group. Gayle Treadwell joined us to bolster our sales and marketing capabilities. With her strong background in the publishing business, she brought many new ideas. As a project manager, we hired a recent master of fine arts graduate, John Cheesman. John brought his knowledge and energy to Oceanview along with the younger generation viewpoint that none of us could provide. That asset proved vital to some of our decision making.

Our daughter-in-law, Diana, was a first year master of fine arts student in the same university program John was finishing. Diana posted our job opportunity notice on the program Web site. After talking with several good candidates from the program, we picked John for the job. A wonderful decision.

Pat's sister, Joanne Savage, in Hendersonville, North Carolina, volunteered her services as an acquisitions editor, to screen the impressive number of electronic submissions that we receive every week from authors and agents. She has amazing literary acumen and she shares our taste in thrillers.

And we recruited volunteer readers to provide opinions about manuscripts that make it through the initial screening. Joanne and this discerning cadre play important roles, but the final decision whether or not to publish each and every title is Pat's and mine.

To the best of our knowledge at the time, we'd now covered all aspects of a publishing company. After only twelve months, Oceanview Publishing was on the map, and books were on the shelves in the bookstores.

Oceanview would concentrate on hardcover books with the idea that they could later be introduced as paperback versions, those larger paperbacks which we call "trade paper" and, we hoped, license the rights for other media. Soon I contracted two New York agencies to handle subsidiary rights: Writers House for domestic rights such as paperback, audio, film, etc., and Waterside Productions in New York and California, to represent us for foreign rights.

Before the end of our first year in business, we learned how difficult it is to predict the success of some key steps. At our request, our New York subsidiary rights agency arranged visits to five of the largest publishing houses in New York, including Random House, Bertelsmann, and Time Warner, so that we could tell their editors our

Oceanview "story," and try to interest them in licensing some of our book list for mass market paperback editions.

We were shocked that editors at these major companies were willing to give us any time at all, but at each house, we were scheduled for a half hour. A couple of days before our trip to Manhattan, Pat suggested that only Sue Greger and I go. Pat could skip it, she felt, because they would give us a few minutes as a courtesy, and she could be more productive in the home office. I argued, successfully as it turned out, that as a partner and our editor in chief, she had to meet those folks and they her.

As we approached the Time Warner skyscraper, I looked up, gestured at the tower and said to Pat and Sue, "That's their company, and right here is ours." We all let out a sort of sickly chuckle. But even just to be accorded an audience was an awesome feeling.

What happened five times in succession astounded us. At each stop, we gave presentations to between two and five senior editors. They had many questions: how we got started, where we found our authors, how we made our editorial decisions. Their main message to us, uniformly, was, *you are doing what we dream of doing.* Publishing good works by talented, but yet-to-be established writers. You're picking your books for quality. We are ruled by our financial colleagues' bottom line, and most books that can make the financial cut over and over again are written by the same few tested, successful authors. The financial folks know these authors do sell and are at very low risk of missing the required sales level. Although at large publishing houses, we still believe in the quality of a new book, it's increasingly difficult to bring in a new or lesser-known author.

These editors pointed out that since our sales requirement obviously was significantly lower than theirs, we could feasibly publish outstanding works by less established or brand-new authors. A couple of the editors even offered to send us manuscripts they loved, but could not get past their financial gatekeepers! At each of the publishers, our presentations and discussions generally lasted more than an hour, and we had to end the meeting so we could go on to our next one.

That tour resulted in a license of one of our books to the Literary Guild, and *Death Angel* by Martha Powers became a "Pick of the Month" for the Doubleday Mystery Book Club. Not bad for an unknown upstart small publisher!

We easily could have talked ourselves out of the visit to the big Manhattan publishers as a no-chance waste of time. But you just cannot always predict the success of a trial balloon you are willing to fly. Moral: optimism and tenacity sometimes do pay off. Serious preparation does help improve the chances.

As we moved through the process toward publishing and selling our first books, we quickly became aware that retirement had vanished. Even our weekends morphed into workdays. But what fun and excitement! We felt like babies learning to walk. Every day, new fun, cool challenges. Please, don't even think of mentioning retirement to Pat. The very word has been retired from her vocabulary.

Chapter Eighteen

Whenever Bob talks about our "retirement," I have to admit I cringe. I don't know why, exactly, and I know that Bob sighs elaborately when I grimace at the word, so I try to cringe inwardly. To me, retirement means just that, you're retired. Put on the shelf, taken out of circulation, over the hill, deleted from the roster because you have nothing more to contribute. I don't like the concept, so I don't like the word.

"Okay, then what word do you like?" Bob says. "How do you want to express your career status?"

"Graduated," I suggest. "Like, I'm a graduate of Johnson & Johnson."

That gets a dismissive smirk.

So I went to *The Synonym Finder* by Jerome Rodale. Retire as a verb: *Withdraw. Go apart. Isolate oneself. Secede. Separate oneself.*

Withdraw? Not how I wanted to spend my life, withdrawing.

Go apart, secede, separate oneself? Well, maybe, but only if departing from something will lead you to something better.

Isolate oneself? Sounds to me like depression.

Rusticate. Hibernate. Estivate. None of these appeal.

Leave. Depart. Decamp. Take off. Go off. Go away. Abscond. Exit. Take one's leave. These descriptors are not too bad, assuming it's your job you're walking away from, and you are walking into a more pleasant life.

Retreat. Fall or draw back. Give way. Lose ground. Take flight. Flee. Beat a retreat. Recede. Retrocede. Ebb. Bury all these loser descriptions! I especially don't like ebb. Why would you ever want to ebb?

More of the synonyms that follow relate to retiring, as in going to bed.

What follow those are even more distasteful synonyms: *Discard. Abandon use of. Disuse. Put on the shelf. Cast aside.* None of the others is cheerful, either.

And we're all clamoring to *retire?*

Graduate, on the other hand, means: *Progression. Succession. Sequence. Continuance. Step-by-step progress.*

Sounds crazy, I'm sure, to say "we graduated" from our company or our careers, but it certainly sounds more optimistic than, "I'm retired." Will somebody please come up with an upbeat, acceptable term? I'm hoping the bureaucrats who design those forms that force pensioners to check the "retired" box can choose a more optimistic descriptor.

I didn't mean to get off track, but I do believe that the concept of retirement, and of all the negativity expressed by the synonymous terms, scares people who are productive, who love to work, and who don't want to end up in the disused or cast-aside category, thank you.

Semantics aside, what Bob and I have entered is a whole new life. And it didn't take long. When we first graduated, both of us were asked to consult for Johnson & Johnson, science and technology — emerging medical technology for Bob, and consumer pharmaceuticals for me. But what we found out after the initial period of about eighteen months was that medical science moves so fast that anything less than total involvement meant we couldn't stay on that razor-thin cutting edge. So consulting became our bridge as we wondered what we'd do next.

But as Bob said earlier, we never explicitly figured it out. Wine and books presented themselves to us. We jumped. Yes, we do still have ties to our former careers. Bob is on corporate, university, and hospital boards. I'm on one corporate board, and I've returned as a volunteer to the first love of my professional life, clinical medicine.

But when I think about it, the vineyards and the publishing company materialized during what, in the moment, we hardly realized was transition time after graduation. Two years went by before we ventured into Oceanview Vineyards, and that probably never would have happened if not for Denis Wade's retirement party in Australia. By the way, Denis never did retire, he's a great example of a fast track graduate, over there in Australia.

From graduation to the germ of Oceanview Publishing spanned about five years, and the motivation wouldn't have surfaced if not for our past professional experiences — starting with writing.

One thing did really lead to another. We talk about our drastic career changes, but the skills and insights gathered over our lifetimes mixed and matched to form the basis for our new endeavors.

Our love for wine and books wasn't enough to provoke all the changes we made after we retired. A couple of years' transition time to the start of a new, fulfilling life was vital, providing a chance to reflect and reevaluate, to listen to our hearts, and appreciate our passions. While we volunteered in clinical medicine and tried out our consulting, we had a chance to consider what we liked and didn't like, to think about how to balance our goals in retirement or graduation. We had to ask ourselves and each other whether we wanted to do *something* or do *nothing* — except retire. Whether we wanted to go for something entirely new or to stick to something we knew well. Work from home or to go to an office? Did we prefer detail-oriented projects, or big-picture strategic ones or both? Did we enjoy working with people or alone? Did we have the financial resources to follow our passions? And maybe

most importantly, in our ideal new world, how do we want
to allocate our time?

These questions were bouncing around in our heads,
more than systematically pondered. At a certain point in
our transition away from science and medicine — after
we'd chosen wine and then books — I did grab a sheet of
paper and begin to list my ideal priorities in our life after
graduation.

Bob's facial expression said he questioned my sanity.
But I kept writing, and I try to stick by what's on that
page. Here's how I try to order my ideal time and energy
investments:

1. Family. My family has always been my highest priority, nothing new there.
2. Healthy lifestyle. A daily work out, minimum
   forty-five minutes when home, together or separately. Either a walk on the beach or on the treadmill.
   We have exercise equipment at home, so we don't
   go to a gym, and so far, we've never had a personal
   trainer, but who knows? Keeping up — literally —
   with the grandchildren, helps, too. Nothing is more
   important than health, and fortunately this retire-
   ment-graduate life phase allows more time to focus
   on staying as healthy as we possibly can.
3. Publishing. As an editor and a publisher, I'm
   conscious of my responsibility to the company and

to each of our authors. I'd never envisioned becoming a writer, much less a publisher, but I chose that responsibility, and once we'd moved into publishing, our company clearly became a priority.

4. Writing. A close second to publishing. Finding this balance makes me feel schizophrenic — in a good way! Ever since I earned my MBA at Columbia while working at Johnson and Johnson, I've loved business. So I love planning, editing, promotion, all the functions that comprise Oceanview Publishing. But even more, I love to write. Now, when I have more than two hours of time to focus, I write. I really look forward to those blocks of time. Not the most efficient approach, certainly, but a necessary compromise.

5. Volunteerism. One of the most attractive features of retirement or graduation is the option to give back to the community. The Senior Friendship Center in Sarasota, Florida, provides health care to lower income seniors and is staffed by volunteer doctors and nurses. As a volunteer primary care physician at the center, I can get back to clinical medicine. A more ideal setting in which to help those who need a doctor most is hard to imagine. For us volunteers, the center provides a deeply rewarding experience. For Bob and me, to serve there is a true privilege.

6. Oceanview Vineyards. A delight! And no wonder,

since our managers in New Zealand do all the heavy lifting in the vineyards, leaving us almost work free on a day-to-day basis. Of course, we are faced with farming executive decisions. Irrigate from the dam or the river? Will the pump make it for one more year? What about the tractor? And on and on, the same as for farmers anywhere. Not to mention all the reports to be evaluated, and, of course, the jaunts to New Zealand to personally check out the progress of the vines.

7. Outside boards. I'm only on one board of directors now — Sarnoff Corporation in Princeton, New Jersey. Sarnoff focuses on high tech innovation, and I find it incredibly inspiring. I decided to drop off the university boards I'd served on when I worked for Johnson &Johnson. Those not-for-profit boards provided a balance, I always felt, between the corporate world and the world of altruism. But in retirement, I wanted to hand off this privilege to the next generation of participants, and to seek out for myself a more hands-on approach to volunteerism.

8. Travel. Bob and I love to travel. Then why did I put it as my last priority? Because, at a certain point, we did make a conscious decision to take our life in new directions. This was our choice. We could have decided to travel more extensively than ever; instead we chose writing and publishing and growing

grapes. Yet we do manage to get around. Yes, there's a lot of business travel, including New Zealand, and we travel back and forth to visit our kids: Florida, Pennsylvania, Michigan, Massachusetts, New York. But Bob and I allow ourselves at least one cruise every year and we visit our favorite island, Anguilla in the Caribbean, every so often. So for an option that ranks at the bottom of an eight-point priorities list, travel doesn't exactly suffer, after all.

Every now and then, I have to take out the list and do a self-assessment. It remains a full list, but one I'm still proud of. It's my personal list. Since Bob first scoffed at my list project, I've never asked him for his. He enjoys living from moment to moment, unencumbered by a priority list. And that's just fine with me.

CHAPTER NINETEEN

Well, now you've heard Pat's list, and you also discovered that I don't have one of my own. Actually, though, I keep Pat's list in my head and follow it as though it were mine. Would that be considered plagiarism? I doubt she'd object!

Pat downplayed the effort required from us in running the vineyards. As she said, we don't do the "heavy lifting," but we do make major business decisions before our contractors proceed. We've changed irrigation systems, constructed equipment sheds, and torn down a house and a sheep-shearing barn on one vineyard, and expanded our planted acreage — "hectares" in New Zealand. All these "heavy-lifting" decisions were ours.

But picture our contractors' wide-eyed stare, when, on a visit during the harvest one year, we told them we did want to participate in the vineyard physical work, as grape pickers. A long moment of silence. The white grapes — sauvignon blanc and chardonnay — are machine harvested, the red pinot noir grapes are handpicked. They knew we wanted to join the hand pickers.

These pickers are an interesting mix of college-age backpackers from around the world, who are looking for a way to make some quick money, and a group of folks our age who more than likely would not be hired for other jobs, but who year after year, participate in the New Zealand grape harvest and are really good at it. As they knew, and we found out, the work is hard.

We inadvertently put on a comedy sketch for the crowd.

When our winery partners met us for breakfast early one morning, they suggested that we buy about fifty large muffins to take to the pickers that morning for their "tea" (we'd call it a coffee break). We left after breakfast, toting three large flat boxes of muffins. When we arrived at the vineyard, the foreman called for all the pickers (about thirty to forty in the crew) to take a break and gather at the edge of the vineyard. He then introduced us as the owners, which drew a round of weak applause. We offered the muffins as our gift, which drew much more vigorous applause.

As the pickers poured themselves tea — or whatever — from their thermoses, and sat on the ground or on portable chairs they'd hauled in for their break, the foreman asked if he could borrow two cutters, like heavy-duty scissors, for Pat and me. Two of the pickers got up and reluctantly handed each of us a cutter, along with a warning about their sharpness. We went forth, and with some instruction from the foreman, proceeded to clip off a few bunches of grapes each. Someone grabbed our camera and recorded the event for posterity. The workers' break lasted about ten minutes and that was the duration of our little show. The owners of the cutters quickly reclaimed their equipment —but not before Pat managed to knick a finger—and returned to the vines.

After feeling the effect on our backs of ten minutes of repeatedly bending over to cut the grape bunches from the vines, we were content with our few bunches each. If the vineyards required as much effort on our part as does the publishing company, we'd be in real trouble.

As Pat told you, we still travel a significant amount for pleasure. In addition to the cruises, both ocean and river, which we really enjoy, we've taken some trips to exotic places like Africa and Antarctica. Out-of-the-ordinary experiences that we highly recommend.

If you do decide to go to Antarctica, prepare for a rough boat ride across the Drake Passage — the turbulent water between Ushuaia, at the southern tip of Argentina, and Antarctica. For us, the passage was thirty-six hours of torture confined to our cabin. We both were repeatedly tossed out of bed by rough seas, and I had several large black-and-blue marks from bumping into the walls and the doorknob on my several excursions to the "head," as they call the bathroom on the ship.

Despite that experience, we encourage anyone who can to see Antarctica while it's still in its unspoiled, beautiful starkness. Don't miss the opportunity to watch the mesmerizing antics of the thousands and thousands of penguins. The males run around gathering stones for the nest as the babies remain in the constant protection of one parent, mother or father — we couldn't tell. We learned that penguins are monogamous, but they have a problem with each other that we have with them. They all look alike and we, and they, can't distinguish one from another. So the poor male, stone in mouth, must run around, lay down the stone and screech for an answer from his particular female. They do, fortunately, recognize each other's calls. We were fascinated to watch the squabbles that ensued when a male tried to steal a stone from another's nest rather than go searching for one on the barren ice fields.

The penguins always seem to march in single file from one location to another. We never could figure out where they were bent on going, except when they marched to the water to dive in, also single file, in search of the krill (tiny shrimp) that they feed on. If the *March of the Penguins* producers could have piped into the theatre the aroma of well-digested and excreted shrimp, the movie would have been oh-so-much more realistic. Even after a week of watching a variety of penguin species, we were still entertained by their activities. They are a sight to behold and one of the highlights of an Antarctica trip.

When we fly to the vineyards in New Zealand, usually we use two or three days during our stay to visit interesting places, either in the country or en route. On our way to New Zealand a few years ago, we stopped at Bora Bora. In this absolutely gorgeous place, we stayed in a thatched-roof hut built over the water, and swam off our private dock. We swam, slept, boated, and ate for an incredibly relaxing few days. Another year we went to Papua, New Guinea, experiencing a remote and still quite undeveloped destination.

The hundreds of Papuan tribes each speak a different language, even though they may only live a few miles apart. Since tribes don't understand each other, generally each stays within its own tribal territory and ventures only short distances. The Sunday market is the great gathering place for each village where residents trade wares. Fish for potatoes, chickens for native crafts — jewelry or pottery, for instance.

We rode in a taxi — an old van, greatly dented and rattling as though it would collapse — driven by a native driver accompanied by his friend as a "guide," to visit a few villages and a Sunday market. At one village that specialized in pottery, we bought a pot.

When we stepped from the van, every woman in the village seemed to emerge from her hut and start putting pots on the ground. Within minutes, we must have been surrounded by two hundred pots. Then an older man, barefoot and shirtless with a cigarette dangling from his mouth, began pointing at pots and shouting at us in a language that we did not understand. The aggressive salesperson for the village was quoting prices. Our "guide" translated prices that ranged from the equivalent of about fifty American cents to two or three dollars.

Pat and I looked at each other and at the pots, wondering what to do. We didn't need a clay pot and we certainly could not haul more than one to New Zealand and back to the U.S. And there sure wasn't any local UPS store. Finally we picked out a pot the size and shape of a bowling ball. It cost about two dollars. No gift wrapping or any wrapping. Dejected women were on their way back to their huts, pots in hand. The disappointed salesman kept shaking his head back and forth as I handed him the baht equivalent of two dollars in payment for the pot. A long ash fell from his cigarette.

When we got back to our hotel, the best available, but not very fancy, a young man was kind enough to wrap the pot for us in newspaper and tape. I suggested to Pat that we buy some sort of bag to carry the round package. In a small outdoor market on the hotel grounds, women were selling handmade scarves and colorful knitted bags with large knitted handles that you could carry in your hand or over the shoulder. Our pot fit perfectly in one of the bags, became easy to handle and would probably survive our travels.

The following day as we approached the small commuter plane to take us back to Port Moresby for our flight to New Zealand, the pilot, who was standing beside the plane, inquisitively pointed to my bag.

"What do you have in there?"

"A pot."

The pilot laughed and informed us that the colorful bags, called billums, are used by the cannibal tribes in the local mountains to carry around the heads of their victims. I must admit that until we were out of Papua, New Guinea, I felt a bit self-conscious about the billum with the round, head-sized, package inside.

Over the years we have made several two to three day trips within New Zealand. We have spent time sightseeing in the city of Auckland, soaking in the hot springs in Rotorua, hiking along the Marlbough Sounds, and we even took a transalpine train ride from the east to the west coast, through the imposing mountains of the South Island, commonly referred to as the Southern Alps.

Both of us love to see new places and meet new people. Our travel often includes several-hour drives around our home in New Zealand, and our homes in the U.S. So, as

Pat said, we still travel a great deal, for pleasure as well as for business.

Now that we've retired — sorry — graduated, and can better control our time, we can do more relaxing travel. We don't plan ever to stop, and we strongly suggest to any of you who have already graduated or will soon, to get started.

Chapter Twenty

When I told Bob I planned to include something here about family, he flinched. Because? He knows I could go on and on about the subject of family and family values. I'll keep it brief.

I began my professional career — in medical school — when I had two children. That was unusual in the sixties. In my class, I was one of a few women, and the only mother. In my neighborhood, I was the only mother who *worked*, though it was actually school, but a demanding program that felt like two jobs, at least.

When I finished medical school, I had four children. I can remember each one's surprise on the day they discovered that so-and-so's mother stayed home all day. Needless to say, I've always had to balance work and family, starting back then — and as my family expanded. That balance goes through many stages, each stage an irreplaceable, precious, and privileged period of time that too quickly becomes a memory. My memories of these stages are vivid, so full of emotion and appreciation. Pregnancy to infancy to toddler to elementary school to middle school to high school and to college. For our kids, that came to twenty colleges and universities. And the final stage is self-sufficiency — assuming all goes well.

Throughout my career, I knew with 100 percent certainty that, if something happened to any one of my children, I would put my career on hold for as long as it took to make sure my family was okay.

Fortunately for us, all did go well. Everybody's healthy. Great careers. Seventeen grandchildren. But my dream always will be for all of them to live in a compound surrounding our house. Independent, but close enough so that all the grandkids could just run in and out and back and forth. Bob's dream — well, maybe he'd put some locks on the doors.

As you can imagine, our kids had a great deal of independence growing up, much more than most kids their age. I think it served them well, and I think that they appreciated their freedom then, and do now. So, in the new millennium, the scary question on each of our children's mind when Bob and I announced our retirement probably was, "Oh my God, what are they going to *do?*" Some of them may have briefly cherished the hope that there'd be abundant babysitting. But in the next moment, they must have begun to develop strategies about passing us from one to the other. Perhaps they'd developed a schedule. A number of days in Boston, before we'd be moved on to Detroit, and then on to Philadelphia. And the two kids that live in Florida, not that far from us, really must have panicked. *Are they going to hang out here all day?*

But to their collective relief, we never moved in with them. We see them often, either at our place or theirs and we have the best of the best grandchildren that we can't wait to see. Yes, seventeen birthdays is a lot to remember, but each is so special. And each child so treasured.

Okay, I'm getting the signal from Bob to stop, but every day, first thing in the morning and last thing at night, I thank God for my family. They are my heart and soul and my inspiration. Bob feels the same way, but at times, he does think I'm a bit excessive. If so, maybe because I grew up with five siblings, and he had only one.

Chapter Twenty-One

While we were building the publishing company, Pat and I continued to make a couple of trips a year to New Zealand to look in on our vineyard. We sold our grapes to two young men, Bruce and Steve, who had started Thornbury Winery. Relatively small but growing, Thornbury was producing some wonderful wines that were sold in many countries.

Their success led the owners to consider moving Thornbury out of their leased space in a large winery, and acquiring their own facility. This would enable their business to grow, they felt, and would provide space and equipment at critical moments in the production cycle. Bruce and Steve always faced problems at harvest time, when their landlord and other winemakers all vied for essential equipment in short supply.

Based on maturity of the crop and the weather, among other factors, the decision to harvest the grapes is difficult, but once made the grapes must immediately be harvested and processed. Grape crushing and harvesting machines are needed only once a season, but when it's time, demand is high and no one can afford to wait. As another company's tenants, Bruce and Steve worried about losing some of the crop when priority for the vital machinery went to others. They felt that they had to have their own facility.

The Thornbury partners owned two vineyards and contracted with five others, including ours. When they were considering ways to generate enough money to enable them to buy land and build their own winery, they requested a meeting with us to discuss an idea.

We could buy one or both of their vineyards, they proposed, and then build a shell on one of them, for use as a winery. They suggested we lease the building back to them on a long-term basis, allowing them to move all of their equipment from their rental space to the new winery. For them, a great plan. To us, a bit scary. Not so much buying a second vineyard, but the thought of owning a winery building.

We analyzed the numbers many times, and finally convinced ourselves that the proposal was feasible, and, with the lease-back agreement, we could afford to do it. We offered to buy one of their two vineyards and build a sheet-metal winery building on the unplanted section. We loved the thirty-acre vineyard—a little smaller than our first one, but at about nine years old, more mature and productive. Another major attraction to us was that it was just behind our villa. We look over the new vineyard from our living room and bedroom windows, and in the distance, a spectacular mountain range. Now we'd be on the stretch of road that connects two major north-south highways and leads to the major route across to the west coast of the South Island. That stretch of road by the vineyard is called "the golden mile." You can understand why we figured that piece of land would be a good investment.

We began the process of purchasing the vineyard, and filed plans for the winery. Such building plans, by New Zealand law, must be announced to the neighbors within a certain distance of the property. A snag. Our neighbors, did not want a winery that close; fearing noise from the equipment and truck traffic, they protested the plan.

Unwilling to alienate our neighbors, we quickly about-faced — but we agreed with our winery partners that we still would buy the vineyard. With cash from the sale, they could proceed with their winery plans at another site; they were pleased. They did find for sale what they declared was an ideal spot for a winery, and the property also would have room enough to plant still more grapes. Then came the kicker. Would *we* consider buying this additional tract, and carry on with the original plan?

We said we would think about it.

Did we need a third vineyard, a fourth property in New Zealand, and a winery? The correct answer was no, but like a kid who's offered a new toy, we were taken with the idea of owning a winery. Only we would know that the "winery" was just a large sheet-metal shed, with electricity, water, and equipment that wasn't ours — and that we had leased it to someone else for twenty years. But we could "romance" our friends, who'd picture a beautiful estate with a large stone building housing a winery, a tasting room, and wine shop, and, of course, a restaurant. Let their imaginations run wild. We wouldn't show them any photos.

Lovely thoughts that led to a crazy decision to say *yes*. We'd proceed toward the purchase of this piece of land, and the winery plans could go forward. The land was only about five miles from our villa and in another beauty spot. We'd romanced *ourselves* into this decision. Less crazy, the American dollar was strong against the New Zealand dollar at that time, which helped.

Then, a reprise. One neighbor, about a half mile from the property, complained about the planned winery. Bruce and Steve negotiated, offered to plant lots of trees around the building, and flowers, to landscape all the property around the winery. They even agreed to paint the building a color suggested by the neighbor couple. But the neighbor would not be satisfied.

Our winery partners went to court and argued that the neighbor's home was so distant that the neighbor could neither see nor hear the winery. Ultimately, our partners gave up the battle, and truth be told, we were relieved. We really did not need the worries of a winery.

The long court battle took a significant financial toll on Bruce and Steve, however, and sapped their energy. They considered an offer from the country's largest, totally New Zealand-owned winery, Villa Maria, to purchase Thornbury. To our astonishment, they accepted the offer and sold the business. We were hardly affected, since Villa Maria now held our supply contract. But we did miss the camaraderie of Bruce and Steve and the fun of working with a small company.

Villa Maria also informed us that they wanted the vineyard we'd planned to buy, which did disappoint us. But we had our own original vineyard, and a large, financially solid winery partner who was contracted to buy our grapes.

Then, about a year later, the unexpected happened yet again. Villa Maria decided they preferred to contract with vineyards, rather than own them. Would we like to buy that vineyard we'd wanted, after all? So eventually we did get our wish and purchased the vineyard bounded by the "Golden Mile," and that we can see from our window. Now we own about seventy acres of vineyard, producing under normal circumstances, over two hundred tons of grapes a year. Not bad for two people whose total knowledge of wine amounts to how much we like to drink it.

We've learned quite a bit, though, over the years,

about growing grapes. We also learned how Mother Nature can turn ugly. Like the frost that destroyed 80 percent of the crop in one of our vineyards in a single night. We happened to be in New Zealand at the time. The day we arrived, we visited that vineyard and it was green, lush, beautiful. Never looked better. The frost that hit that night was only one degree below frost level.

When we returned the following day, the vineyard looked as though a fire had come through. Black vine leaves crumbled in your hands. Shocked, we were reminded of late fall vistas in Pennsylvania.

To our relief, we learned that, long term, the vines would recover; their yield might be a little lower than normal the following year. That same year's crop, of course, was a different story. Our respect grew dramatically for farmers and their tricky partnership with Mother Nature.

So today we have Oceanview Vineyard, Renners Road; Oceanview Vineyard, Rapaura Road; and Oceanview Publishing. Wow, can we refer to the group as Oceanview Industries? Probably, not quite.

Chapter Twenty-Two

Lest you think that our hectic work schedule might be hazardous to our health, I assure you it's not. As Pat told you, we have workout equipment in our Hamptons house; and, our condominium in Florida has a wonderful fitness facility. When we're not traveling, we work out every day — and many days when we are. And we enjoy the results.

On my sixty-ninth birthday, I weighed 197 pounds and my waist was just north of forty inches. When I bent over, I could hardly breathe. A year later, I weighed 163 pounds and my waist was thirty-four inches. I'd say I'm in better physical condition now than I've been since college.

How? By reducing food portions by about one-third (and you can be sure they're still sufficient), limiting carbohydrate intake, plus a vigorous daily workout of from forty-five minutes to an hour. Each day I run/walk two to two-and-a-half miles on a treadmill at a 3 to 5 percent uphill grade, do one hundred to one hundred twenty-five crunches for the "abs" and spend about fifteen minutes pumping on a weight machine and with free weights.

In high school, I never weighed more than 140 pounds, even though I ate everything I could get my hands on, trying to get to a reasonable football playing weight. No success there. Then, for totally mysterious reasons, in my junior year in college, my weight shot up to 187 pounds, to go *up* from there, but never down, until my seventieth birthday. According to the actuarial charts, the ideal weight for a man my height is 158 pounds. I'm just about there.

A shame, I guess, that it took me so long to get smart and fit. But the upside to being out of shape for fifty years is that when you get back in condition at a more advanced age, you feel extra great. I'm no fitness expert, but I need to be the one to tell you I have not felt this good in years.

For those who have graduated, and who now have more time, my advice is spend some of that time improving your physical condition. Exercise, watch your diet. My example says the results will be worth the effort.

A word from Pat: Yes!

I do agree with everything Bob said about diet and exercise. Personally, I'm a longtime advocate of the low-carbohydrate diet. Remember the era when nutritionists, outraged by the anti-carbohydrate contingent, preached low fat, high-carbohydrate diets? Now, ten short years later, we know that, for effective weight loss and general health promotion, low-carbohydrate diets outperform low-fat diets.

Let me give you my take on exercise: Yep. Exercise is important. Promotes health and wellness in so many ways. That you already know. What I do want to say, though, is that I think exercise is horribly boring. If you're an aerobic sports type, a swimmer or tennis player or even a golfer, then it's probably fun for you. Except I could never understand how swimming could be *not* boring. So that leaves those of us, not especially athletic, not especially motivated folks, who can think of almost anything else we'd love to do to avoid exercise.

Well, I found the answer. Something that works for me where nothing else ever has. I have to admit that, with a career and a big family, I never had time for entertainment. That means I have inadequate knowledge of all things to do with movies and TV shows. Well, except the seventies kids' shows. I'm bad with the "pinks" of Trivial Pursuit. But that's all changing now, as I load up my DVD player with a movie from NetFlix.

When I'm choosing a movie, or better yet, when I'm in the middle of watching a movie, I can't wait to hit the "torture" machines. On the treadmill or the stationary bike, I watch movies. And time, as they say, flies. It really does. Often, I find myself going way past my mandatory forty-five minutes because I'm enthralled by the movie. I just can't stop. A good thing for your body. So after all these years, I'm catching up on movies. All I need is a DVD player connected to a TV, or a standalone player that's my fallback when I'm not at home. Music is good, too, but I find that time slips away faster when I'm watching a movie, especially a thriller.

So a diet low in carbohydrates with reasonable portions combined with exercise plus a movie seems a good prescription for health and wellness. And we know where a healthy lifestyle is on my priorities list.

Oh, the wine. Yes! With all its lovely health benefits. Red for me, Villa Maria pinot noir, of course. Bob prefers white wine, Villa Maria sauvignon blanc from our New Zealand vineyards, naturally.

Chapter Twenty-Three

People regularly ask, "When did you retire, Pat?" Sounds like an innocent question, but hearing the "R" word spoken in the same sentence as "you" that actually refers to *me* still makes me wince. I know, it's a stupid hang-up and maybe someday I'll get over it. I answer the question, but I always feel compelled to add, "My husband and I retired in the year two thousand, *on the same day*."

For the people who know Bob, that might be an interesting tidbit of information. But perfect strangers must wonder, "Why would she say that?"

For a woman with a career and a husband, the question of *retirement* — okay, let's just call it that, for now — is complex. But for a woman who has not worked outside the home, I can only imagine that the specter of her husband's retirement must strike terror. Picture one's perfectly organized life disrupted, turned upside down, cluttered with unwanted disturbances, upset by unknown intrusions to come. I can only guess here, since I've never had to face that scenario, yet. I suppose Bob could decide to drop out of the wine and book businesses, and leave me toiling away while he putters about the house and devotes himself, full-time, to his *food impressionism*.

For us, the whole retirement scenario began with him. A corporate officer at Johnson & Johnson was more or less expected to retire at age sixty-two. Dutifully, two years in advance, Bob told the CEO that he planned to do just that. Later when they asked him to stay another year, he declined. So where did that leave me? I loved my job.

Bob had worked for the same corporation for twenty-six years, and I had worked for that same corporation for twenty-four years. Though it may have been a bit unusual in the seventies for a married couple to work in the same corporation, our experience couldn't have been better. The corporation got its money's worth from us as we spent lots more time talking about work issues — and consider the savings in health benefits — two for the price of one, almost.

We ended up in different operating companies — Johnson & Johnson has more than two hundred operating units — but we were both in the research and development side of the business. Bob was at corporate in New Brunswick, New Jersey; I was in consumer pharmaceuticals in Fort Washington, Pennsylvania. Usually, we went our separate ways, doing our own thing, but on occasion we'd find ourselves seated at the same table, representing our separate business interests at the same meeting; and, of course, we knew a lot of the same J&J people. There also were occasions, nice for us, when we both were called to attend company meetings in exotic places.

So when Bob chose his retirement date, announcing it two years in advance, I had no idea what I would do. But one day soon after his choice, during a meeting with my boss and my boss's boss about department salaries and promotions, I blurted, "I've decided to retire in twenty-four months."

I don't know who was more shocked, me or they — or Bob, when I told him later that night. But now, years later, I know the decision was right, and one I've never regretted, not for a minute.

What I think drove me to that decision, seemingly impetuous, but one that must have been working in my subconscious is that I must have been imagining. Imagining Bob *not* getting up before the crack of dawn, leaving for his office in suit and tie, to arrive before the starting bell — for Bob, *on time is late.* Imagining Bob *not* going to all his meetings, *not* assisted by his *assistant,* the indispensable Michelle Noval. Not juggling a hectic travel schedule.

Many women are blessed with husbands who are handy

guys, who relish the chance to tear down a wall, rip apart a bathroom, or put in another staircase. But this was not Bob. He can hang paintings, change lightbulbs, even do the odd caulking job, but I don't think he enjoys it. Just once, for reasons unknown to me, he decided to install a large, ornate chandelier over our foyer by himself. First, the ceiling was so high, and Bob does not like heights. The project included new electrical connections, a dimmer, a two-way switch, and I don't know what all. I really was scared when he flipped the switch. I couldn't believe my eyes, when — without electrocuting himself or setting the house on fire — the lights twinkled on, setting the hallway and foyer aglow. Sadly, this was the first and last demonstration of such do-it-yourself talent. In Bob's retirement, I suspected, routine trips back and forth to Home Depot were unlikely.

What *would* Bob do all day? Wander the house aimlessly? Take up daytime television and become absorbed in the soaps, or all that reality stuff? He'd mentioned once in a while that he wanted to paint, as in be an artist. Would he settle down at an easel with pastels or oils or watercolors? Would he spend all day shopping for the perfect ingredients for his emerging cooking obsession? He'd already taken over the kitchen, and losing that turf was fine with me, but suppose he did zero all day, except ponder what to cook for dinner?

I couldn't begin to fathom all that. Much less, what

would he do when I went off on business trips? What would *I* do when he went off on pleasure travel *without* me? So many questions. So many possibilities. I guess I figured whatever was going to happen, I wanted to be part of. So, I said, "*Me*, too."

Plus, I wanted to move forward toward a writing career. The only realistic, pragmatic way for me to pursue my newfound passion was to make time for it. Something had to give. So I jumped with both feet into retirement, right along with Bob. Back then, I expected to be writing full time; how could I know that wine and publishing would intervene. But I do make enough time to write, and my work as editor in chief for Oceanview Publishing has taught me more about writing than I ever could have predicted. And, you might not be surprised to hear, drinking Villa Maria wine has been a definite plus.

CHAPTER TWENTY-FOUR

We're still astonished that in the year two thousand, we had no inkling of a future either in book publishing or the wine business. We volunteered in a clinic and a hospice — we still do, we consulted for Johnson & Johnson, and we served on university and corporate boards in the medical-scientific field. These activities grew out of and relied on our education and background.

Today, we grow grapes, write novels, and publish books. How did we get *here*, we marvel. You've heard something about that chain of events. Are we happy? We love it. We could not be happier.

We still keep up with medical and scientific journals, we go to medical meetings periodically, and when we are in Florida, as a part of our clinical medicine volunteer activity, we take part in hospital grand rounds on Friday mornings, and go to healthcare lectures at our low-income seniors' clinic.

Do we miss our former careers? Not really. We miss so many of the J&J people, and collaborating with them. But we still see old friends and colleagues, and we've met so many new ones. Our publishing company team provides the closeness of a cohesive work group and a diversity of personalities that makes every day a pleasure.

The only downside? We work seven-day-a-week jobs now. But what great fun, and how incredibly stimulating to learn new things every day about viticulture and about literary talent. From medicine and scientific research to books and wine has been a voyage full of new kinds of fun and excitement for us — not to mention a wonderful sense of accomplishment.

Our publishing company's goal — helping authors and bringing new ones onto the literary scene, which we accomplish all the time, is most rewarding. So between publishing, board participation, and our volunteerism, we feel we are giving something back.

We do work long hours, but now we can control our time much better than when we were in our "original" careers. In our own business, we also can surround ourselves with our choice of interesting and energetic and innovative people. A luxury, needless to say, you don't always have when you work in the mainstream of industry.

Life is too short to just stop contributing, and the post-graduation years are the perfect time to follow your passion. One step at a time. Or, just plunge in.

Chapter Twenty-Five

Many people tell us they can't believe that after so many years in our original professions we were able, in so few years, to move into totally new and unrelated careers. But how? And isn't it frightening? Don't you miss your old life? Have you given up all recreation? And so on.

Well, now, from our story, you've got an idea of the *how*.

Are all those changes scary? A little, but we are more amazed and exhilarated than frightened. As to recreation, we still vacation, visit the kids and they visit us, we play tennis and golf periodically, ride bikes, work out, swim, even read books for pleasure. We've graduated to a different, always full, life. We wouldn't trade it for retirement.

And then we get to that popular question, so often asked: Do you think that we (or I), the questioner wants to know, could change the direction of our (my) life to that same extent?

Once again, *yes.*

But everyone has their own index of tolerance for change — some go for avoidance, to the extent possible — others thrive on change. Most of us look for a balance, a transition from incremental putting your toe in the water to a complete plunge. But the trick is to identify the jumping off point. Listen to your heart and balance your passion with your skills and your financial status. Some changes do require more financial input and risk than others, and everyone has to consider their own ability to take on new and different activities. Examine your wishes and fears, consider the pros and cons of your options, and then start the next chapter of your life.

A great story of changing the direction of one's life at an advanced age, despite modest means, is my Aunt Alice's. When my dad was thirteen and Alice was eleven, they were orphaned in their native Russia as the Bolshevik revolution raged. A network of friends and relatives quickly and quietly spirited the two youngsters out of Russia, through Europe, to London. They were to board a ship to the United States, to live with relatives in Detroit. But Alice contracted measles and was quarantined in London, causing a six-month delay before they could be put on a ship bound for the United States.

Upon arrival in Detroit, Michigan, they settled in with relatives. Their aunts and uncles put them to work doing chores and generally serving the homeowners. Their formal education was over.

After a few years, Alice found work in a local laundry and stayed on in the relatives' home, but my father left for New York and a series of jobs. He and my mother met, the story goes, at a wedding in Toledo, Ohio; eventually they married and settled in Pittsburgh, Pennsylvania.

Aunt Alice was in her early twenties when she met and married Max, a Detroit barber. She lived her life in Detroit, as a stay-at-home mother who raised three children, loved to cook and garden, but never ventured far, and never even learned to drive a car. She was wonderful to me, and I loved my visits to her comfortable, welcoming home — especially frequent when I was a hungry college guy at the University of Michigan.

But Alice's idyllic life came to an abrupt halt with Max's sudden death at age fifty-nine. Alice's metamorphosis began; she was sixty years old.

She took driving lessons and got her license — but only after taking the test three times because her English comprehension wasn't up to some of the questions on the written exam. But she did get her license. Then she found a job in a nursing home, caring for the residents. She worked full time, driving to and from her job five days a week, even in the extreme winter weather of the Midwest. When Alice reached sixty-five, the nursing home management brought up the subject of retirement. She ignored them, but when she reached seventy, the union finally forced her out.

No retirement for Alice. She searched for another job, even going to a vocational center; she assured them she was happy to be trained for any kind of job. In short order, a jewelry store hired Alice, now seventy years old. She cleaned showcases, swept the floor, made coffee, and did every odd chore requested of her, or that she decided needed to be done. Needless to say, the owners loved her. This lasted for several years, even as the owners, concerned about her driving in poor weather, urged her to retire. Just short of her eightieth birthday, she finally agreed to give up the jewelry store job. The owners sent her on a three-day Las Vegas vacation, with a tidy sum in gambling money.

But Alice returned from Vegas still unwilling to retire. Back to the vocational center she went for more training. They convinced her, rather than go back out to work this time, to take drawing and painting classes. To everyone's surprise, she showed talent. She could really draw. And draw she did. And paint. She fell in love with painting clowns, pets, and various cartoon characters.

Alice finished almost a hundred paintings over the next several years. Though she specialized in clowns, she'd ask children to give her a photo of a pet, or a favorite cartoon character, and she'd draw and paint from the photo and give the child the framed artwork.

She learned to crochet, too, and she provided every relative, friend, and neighbor with an afghan. Incredibly kind and generous, she always was available to drive friends to shops, to the doctor, or wherever they had an errand. When Aunt Alice died in her late eighties, she left a legacy not only of the charming, cheery paintings and the afghans, but of encouragement. She was a model of how amazing changes can be accomplished, even late in life. Who could forget a story like Aunt Alice's? She was an inspiration to me, to her children, and surely to anyone who had the good fortune to meet her.

A chance encounter on an airplane provided another graphic example of a radical change in life direction. We already were immersed in our publishing venture when I was flying to Texas for the meeting of a hospital board on which I still serve. I finished reading a manuscript I'd brought with me and, since I'd left the rest of my reading material in my checked suitcase, I closed my eyes and tried to grab a quick nap. Although I felt sleepy enough, I just could not fall asleep.

I happened to notice that the relatively young fellow seated next to me was reading a veterinary journal. He had a second journal and I asked him if I might take a look at it. Politely, he handed me a journal for veterinary technicians. Was he a veterinarian or a veterinary tech? I inquired. Then I heard his story. Not his real name, but let's call him "Joe."

Joe was forty-eight years old, he told me, and had just been laid off from his job in the printing shop where he'd worked for fifteen years. Because of a business slowdown, the family owned company had let go eleven people, including Joe. He always knew he wouldn't advance in the firm — and was really bored with his job — still, he'd fully expected to work there until retirement.

Distraught about being out of work at age forty-eight, Joe had called his sister in Seattle, Washington, with his news. His sister was bright and entrepreneurial, he told me — she and another woman had built a successful environmental consulting company. Her advice: Joe should look into retraining in a field where job opportunities were good — and where they likely would stay that way. The veterinary field, for instance.

Joe listened to his sister, and did some research. A community college near his home in Tampa, Florida, offered a two-year program toward an associate degree as a veterinary technician. Joe decided to enroll. He had saved some money during his years at the printing company. Then he found a veterinary hospital near his home where he volunteered, with the hope of getting part-time employment later, to help pay for his degree.

When we met on the plane, Joe had been working at the animal hospital for about two months, and soon would start the technician program. Joe said he could not wait to get to the hospital each day; he was excited every morning when he awoke. He loved every task he was given by the vets and by the other technicians. He devoured the journals, and the more he learned, the happier he felt.

Still, Joe said, he worried about whether he could really make such a drastic change at this stage of his life, and be successful. I told him about Pat and me.

Our story really inspired him, Joe told me, and boosted his confidence that he could succeed in his new life. I agreed that indeed he could, and that he had every reason to wake up excited each day to pursue his new challenges.

Just another example of how, regardless of limited circumstances or how old you are, you can change direction and end up satisfied and successful.

People have shared with us so many stories about the process of change, about how they took hold of their life and turned it in the new direction prompted by their heart and passion. The outcome, in case after case, was success well beyond their dream. Stories of failure may be out there, but few compared to all the tales of success.

I can't resist just one more. During our periodic trips to our favorite island, Anguilla, in the Caribbean Sea, we've became acquainted with the Blanchards, Bob and Melinda. Proprietors of Blanchard's restaurant, they tell the surprising and inspiring story of their life direction changes in two books: *A Trip to the Beach: Living on Island Time in the Caribbean* and *Live What You Love*. The Blanchards certainly faced challenges, but they've enriched their lives, and, like us, they chose a direction that has taken them to places literally, as in geographically, they never could have imagined.

Pat and I highly recommend these books about life changes — as well as the Blanchards' culinary books. If you get to Anguilla, you must go to Blanchard's. The restaurant is one of the tops on an island that is rich with outstanding eating establishments. And while you're there, take the opportunity to talk with this fascinating couple.

Chapter Twenty-Six

Can anyone do what we and Aunt Alice and "Joe" and the Blanchards have done? Move from one career to totally different and unrelated activities? Particularly, can the move be made at a more advanced age, even in retirement?

We don't claim to be experts on this phenomenon. But we are a real-life example. We made our drastic changes in this retirement/graduation stage of our lives. And we managed it all in not so many years. We jumped into areas as far removed as you could imagine from our original careers and field of activity. And within five years of retirement, we'd successfully changed direction and safely arrived. So retirement is gone — for now. We simply shifted gears and went on in new directions. Or, as Pat would say, we graduated again.

Did we have to be retired, though, to make the choices and changes we made? In fact, when we looked back at our lives, we realized that we made some pretty drastic changes long ago. When we finished our formal education and training, Pat went into private practice and I went into research and teaching on a medical school faculty. Each of us intended to stay in these roles for our entire career. But fate intervened. Each of us received and accepted offers to join the pharmaceutical industry in research roles. Each thought the new opportunity sounded interesting, but that after gaining some unique additional experience, we'd probably return to our former positions. Instead, we spent the rest of our careers in the healthcare products industry. The challenges were interesting and the field exciting; we felt we made valuable contributions toward disease cures and prevention, and better overall health in the U.S., and in countries around the world.

We notice, looking back, that both of us practiced what much later we called *thoughtful impulsiveness*. We took a chance, we tried something new. We may have surprised ourselves, I guess, with our willingness to adopt different roles and become passionate all over again. But having worked a combined total of more than fifty-five years in our medical research jobs, obviously we loved that field, and would not trade those careers for anything.

People can change jobs or even careers. It may take some *thoughtful impulsiveness* such as we displayed in many of our decisions. Sometimes the impulsiveness may not have been so thoughtful! But to make significant changes in job, career, or even life, does take some impulsiveness.

People often analyze, think and frighten themselves out of making these kinds of changes. We put it this way: *Thoughtful impulsiveness conquers procrastination and paralysis by analysis.* Why should age be an obstacle to life change? Medical and nutritional advances allow us to stay much healthier as we get older. From a fitness and health standpoint, today's sixty-year-old is the forty-year-old of twenty-five years ago. And fresh challenges seem to be beneficial as we grow older, in maintaining sharp minds.

Naturally, some people are happy pursuing less challenging lifestyles. We love to travel — many retirees make travel a full-time occupation. Others are thrilled to be able to play golf or tennis every day or go fishing or just relax. "Different strokes," as the saying goes, "for different folks."

CHAPTER TWENTY-SEVEN

Most of us start thinking about retirement between ages forty and forty-nine, according to a *Wall Street Journal* report on a Harris interactive online survey. Retirement planning, the article explains, is not just a financial matter, but a lifestyle issue. The poll posed the questions: What do people want to do in retirement? How do they want to spend their time?

Seventy-one per cent of those surveyed said they'd like to work after retirement from their primary career. But only 5 percent say they'd want to work full time. The rest, 26 percent, want to work part time, and 40 percent want to alternate between periods of work and leisure.

These responses bring to mind two questions. Is the decision to work full time or part time driven by a need for more income, more financial security? Or are we driven by a need to spend time doing something of interest? Or both?

Financial security is, to some extent, measurable. All kinds of advisors can estimate how much money you'll need to support your lifestyle in retirement. But if you're fortunate enough to have adequate resources to see you through your retirement years without your having to work for a paycheck, the consideration becomes, "what do you *want* to do?" So, we face some decisions.

For some, doing little or being reactive is their preference. They've worked hard all their lives, they just want to kick back and go with the flow. Provided that's what they do want — wonderful! Others love what they've been doing, and prefer to continue at some level, even well into retirement, perhaps for their entire life. Significant directional life change isn't for everyone. Another group may dream of doing something truly different, but fear making the change.

What's important is to follow your passion and be open to moving out of your comfort zone, into something completely new. Make excitement, satisfaction, and happiness your goal. Our prediction is that you'll find opportunities you never could have anticipated.

Having read our story, you know that everything doesn't follow from one big epiphany. For us, the first breakthrough was Pat's writing, and later, mine. Followed by the unthinkable — a vineyard we literally stumbled into — and then came the publishing company: full circle back to the writing. All this was made possible by what we now call, *thoughtful impulsiveness*. The first example for us, looking back, was probably buying that property in the Hamptons.

Have we made some mistakes? You bet! Have we been faced with disappointments? A few, but they've been over-shadowed by the delights and the excitement. Hard work? Harder than we could have imagined. Remember the seven-day work weeks and the long hours. Are we happy we did it? Ecstatic!

Here's the last word. *Yes.* From Pat. She always gets the last word.

Will we make another directional change? Will there be a post-graduation life stage? A couple of months ago, Bob announced, "I've decided to give away our golf clubs. We haven't used them recently. Guess I'll give them to one of the kids or grandkids."

Was I hearing things? "What? Give away our golf clubs!"

In fact, we hadn't played in a couple of years. Not that we'd ever played regularly, so it wasn't like we'd dropped a favorite hobby. Besides, I'd had foot surgery the year before, and Bob had both his knee and shoulder repaired.

"We're never going to play," Bob said, with what I perceived as a pout.

Uh-oh. Maybe golf actually had migrated onto Bob's secret priority list and we should make an adjustment.

"But we need them," I said. My thought was, *we'll need them when we move into the next stage.* Golf sounds like a good idea for the next stage. Right now, we seem on the busy side to spend five hours or more of our week on the golf course, but still, I reacted to Bob's plan for the golf clubs.

"We'll play tomorrow."

And we did, and had a great time, and will do it more often. But not every week.

Finding the right balance time-wise and job-wise is the tricky part. Significant directional life change isn't for everyone. But for those who think — *maybe?* — our experience says, give it a try. Open your mind. Follow some whims. Go with thoughtful impulsiveness. Most of us can do much more than we ever imagined. But whatever you decide to do, be sure to have fun. If you're not having fun, change again. As long as life is, it is not long enough to be unhappy with what you're doing.

Take it from two happy and energized people: you, too, can enjoy a chance to look back one day, fascinated with the question, *How did we get here?* And ask the question, *What's next?*